A SHANTY TOWN
IN SOUTH AFRICA

ANDREW SILK

A SHANTY TOWN
IN SOUTH AFRICA

THE STORY of MODDERDAM

RAVAN PRESS   **JOHANNESBURG**

Published by Ravan Press (Pty) Ltd.
409 — 416 Dunwell, 35 Jorissen Street,
Braamfontein, Johannesburg 2001, South Africa.
First Impression 1981
© Copyright Andrew Silk
Photographs: *The Argus, The Cape Times*, Gavin Younge
Typesetting: Sandy Parker
Cover photograph: Franco Frescura
Design: The Graphic Equalizer

ISBN 0 86975 193 X

Printed by The Mafeking Mail, Roodepoort.

To the people of Modderdam:
n'kosi 'nKulu

Acknowledgement

In researching and writing this book, I have received invaluable assistance from organizations, friends, and colleagues in the United States and South Africa.

The Thomas J Watson Foundation provided the grant for me to visit South Africa. The Urban Planning Research Unit of the University of Cape Town provided funding for an unpublished series of interviews with African workers which I have drawn upon for background. The Institute for Social Development at the University of the Western Cape and the Cape Flats Committee for Interim Accommodation, which is now disbanded, were both extremely helpful in introducing me to the residents of Modderdam. While the research would not have been possible without the assistance of these groups, the book was conceived and written independently.

Questions suggested by Prof Philip Mayer helped direct some of the interviews at Modderdam. An article by Prof Mayer, drawn from parts of the research, appeared in the *Eastern Province Herald*, August 27, 1977.

I have been inspired by Francis Wilson's searching investigations into the migrant labour system and by his personal support for this book.

Gail Gerhart, Tom Karis, Wendell Pietersen, Patrick Harries, Martin Kessler, William Shawn, Mark Silk, Tema Silk, Adam Silk, and Greg Tobin have all discussed the book with me and read the manuscript at different stages. Their broad reading and experience helped me to focus and shape the material.

Nancy Perlman and my parents, Leonard and Bernice Silk, were understanding supporters and demanding critics.

I owe my greatest debt to friends in South Africa, both in and outside Modderdam, who asked to remain anonymous. I look forward to the day when these men and women will feel free to tell their stories openly.

Contents

Preface

Two bulldozers knocked down the homes of ten thousand black South Africans on a patch of land twelve miles east of Cape Town during the week of August 8, 1977. The homes were shanties of corrugated iron, plastic, wood and cardboard built on sandy ground cleared of small trees and thick brush. The camp was called 'Modderdam' because it lay on Modderdam Road, a two-lane parkway east of Cape Town on the Cape Flats, a short isthmus which links the city to the continent. The residents were illegal squatters. Visitors to the shanty town they had built were told: 'We took a piece of land from the white man.'

After the police raided one rainy night — firing shots in the air and arresting men and women — the community organized. A committee was formed to govern the town and defend the camp. For months, the squatters lived by their own laws, under their own leaders, and the camp became a twenty-acre sanctuary from white rule.

The government first ordered most of the men of the camp into nearby hostels, and the women and children to rural villages. When the families refused to disperse, the government came to see Modderdam as a threat to its authority. White clergymen and community workers, black students and migrant workers were all drawn into the conflict. The squatters and their supporters used stones, weighted sticks, knives, demonstrations, fasts, petitions and law suits as they battled in the bush, the schools, the newspapers, the courts, and in Parliament.

As the camp was razed, squatters chanted hymns and freedom songs, charged columns of policemen, and hurled furniture onto

Modderdam Road. Many burnt down their own shacks. Police used dogs and teargas to disperse the crowds of hymn-singers, spectators, and demonstrators. Several squatters were hospitalized with dog bites. One woman, treated for chest pains, was discharged from the hospital back to the camp with instructions to rest in bed for two weeks. Two women in labour were rushed to an emergency room. A third gave birth to a girl under a plastic tarpaulin next to the sidewalk. As a bulldozer approached one shack, a government official heard a baby scream. He ran into the shanty and yanked a two-week old boy from his mother's arms. 'God knows it is an inhumane task,' he told a reporter as he cuddled the child, 'but I am trying to make it as humane as possible.'

There were no deaths.

The squatters slowly left the camp once their 'pondoks' were down. A few accepted free rail tickets to villages several hundred miles away. Many more moved in with friends and relatives in shanty towns and brick townships nearby. A large number were put in tents erected on house and church lawns in the white sections of Cape Town. An anti-government community organization protested the demolition by placing five families within full view of the Parliament buildings on the grounds of St George's Cathedral. Passers-by on their lunch hour flipped snacks to the mothers and their children over an iron fence. The police later confiscated the tents and arrested their inhabitants.

The destruction of Modderdam was a culmination of the continual struggle of the white South African government to keep African families out of Cape Town. At the height of the battle, the milkmen, nightwatchmen, housewives, construction workers, gardeners and unemployed people who lived in the shanty town were briefly at the centre of black resistance in the country. When the camp was lost, many squatters became increasingly dependent on white charity. Few left Cape Town. In the end, as in the beginning, the squatters were left searching for land.

This book is the story of the people who came to Modderdam and of their fight to keep their homes. Throughout most of the narrative, I have stuck closely to a description of the characters and events in and around the shanty town.

Yet the story goes beyond the camp's narrow boundaries. For the contradiction which forms the central thread in the life of the squatters is also woven through South African history. The economy's huge appetite for black labour is in conflict with white fears of being 'swamped', then ruled by blacks. Modderdam was a microcosm of this classic struggle.

A squatter camp may seem a poor vehicle through which to examine a central force in South African society. Chronic housing shortages throughout Africa, Asia and Latin America have made shanty towns commonplace in the Third World, and the penchant for bulldozing them is not uniquely South African. In Kinshasa, Zaire, shanty towns lining the road to the airport are routinely knocked down to prepare for the arrival of a prominent head of state. Elsewhere, the dispersal of squatters is seen as a stiff cure to unemployment.

Modderdam, however, differed from these shanty towns because the South African government *did* have the resources to provide solid housing. Unlike squatters elsewhere, most men at the camp were working. They sought the most basic city goals — the right to live with their families in flimsy shacks and work in menial jobs. They saw their towns as an assertion that they would no longer be denied the family life, medical care and food available in Cape Town. Their struggle to obtain these modest demands was a test of black South Africa's ability to win the greater struggle for acceptance in the city.

The fundamentals of this fight could be seen at the camp without distortion because there were no martyrs there. The men and women who fought to keep the camp were hardly known outside Modderdam and were forgotten after they had left. The building of the camp was overshadowed by the June, 1976 uprising which began in Soweto. The demolition was eclipsed by the death in detention of young black leader Steve Biko. Modderdam's relative obscurity made it possible to see basic and practical issues which might have been overlooked in an international campaign.

I stumbled onto this story of a South African shanty town. I had first worked in South Africa in 1974, as a visiting reporter on *The Pretoria News*. When I returned two years later, I intended to gather an oral history of apartheid, speaking with blacks and whites throughout the country. It was for this purpose that I first visited the camp in February, 1977. I had originally planned to conduct only a few interviews there, yet after a week, I decided to spend

3

as much time at Modderdam as possible. Shortly after I had begun to interview at the camp, an African community worker arrived to conduct research there as well. We decided to work together and interviewed over thirty squatters and came to know a few of the residents as friends.

During these weeks in the camp, the government was restrained by a court order from any demolition. The police permitted visitors a relative freedom to enter Modderdam. A white official once asked me to leave, but when I returned the next day with a group of social work students, he said nothing. As Modderdam was not a legal African township, whites needed no permit to enter.

It was difficult to predict who in the camp would be anxious to talk, who would refuse, and who would simply nod their heads to our questions. I feared initially that I would be looked upon as an official, even though white volunteers were frequently in the camp. Yet once I was formally introduced to the squatters during their Sunday meeting, I was seldom questioned.

We spoke to men and women of different generations, backgrounds, and legal categories. Most interviews were conducted through simultaneous translation in Xhosa and English for about an hour, although there were a few which each of us did alone. I then transcribed and lightly edited the transcripts. Where accounts overlapped, I have taken some details from one story and included it in the second, rather than repeating both full interviews.

I was surprised by the honesty and openness of so many of the residents. This, I suspect, had little to do with their trust in me or my African colleague. So many were so desperate and so tired that it no longer mattered to them what they said or to whom they said it. The most representative of these accounts appear in Part I of the book.

I later explored the history of South Africa's industrial revolution and the development of the laws regulating African movement and came to see how central the squatter's experience was to the growth of the South African economy. The historical account presented in Part II mirrors the squatters' own description of the evolution of apartheid.

As the struggle for the camp intensified during 1977, Modderdam became a test of the government's efforts to keep recent black immigrants from settling in the city. And when the churches, the opposition press, and other organizations supported the squatters, the campaign revealed both the strength and cleavages within the opposition. Part III is an account of that campaign.

The destruction of the camp and its bizarre aftermath (Part IV) provided a glimpse of the chaos and strife which is inevitable as long as the government clings to apartheid's fundamental principle and refuses to grant blacks full rights to travel, settle, seek work, buy land, and ultimately, vote in the city.

Three years after Modderdam was demolished, the plight of some Cape Town squatters has improved. The Minister for Plural Relations, Piet Koornhoof, in late 1978 abruptly halted the demolition of Crossroads, Cape Town's last African shanty town. After a long campaign, the camp is still standing and has been proclaimed an African township. Many squatters will receive permits to stay in the city, and will gradually be moved into brick homes in the neighbouring township, Nyanga.

At the same time, however, the government has increased penalties and restrictions on all future immigrants. The policy is yet another attempt to draw the final line of African settlement. Hunger, sickness, and unemployment, though, grow ever deeper in the rural areas. Unless reform extends much further, there will be many more Modderdams.

Andrew Silk
Norfolk, Virginia
August 1980

PART 1
The Squatters Arrive

1. A Liberated Zone

The shanties of Modderdam were surrounded by the fine beaches, lush vineyards and gentle mountains of the Cape Peninsula, as well as by the drab, regimented, black townships of the Cape Flats. Seeds of the confrontation between the squatters and the government lay in the camp's setting.

The grace of the Atlantic and Indian Ocean shores and the Mediterranean climate give the Peninsula a slightly sleepy air, seemingly removed from the tumult of life in South Africa. The modest gables of the Cape Dutch homes are displayed on the slopes and in the valleys of Table Mountain to the west and the Hottentot-Hollands chain to the east — about twelve miles on either side of the ground where Modderdam was built.

Modderdam was in black Cape Town. The African townships of Nyanga, Guguletu and Langa were about five miles away, their long rows of brick 'matchbox' houses a dull contrast to the jagged, flimsy shacks of the camp. The 'coloured' township of Elsie's River was a short walk from the shanty town, the monotony of its crowded neighbourhoods broken in part by the frenzy of the outdoor markets along the main road.

Several government-supported 'showcase' buildings for 'coloureds' stood at Modderdam's immediate borders. Belhar, the newest and most attractive coloured housing development on the Flats, lay across the railroad tracks. The new homes, lawns, and gardens together make up a suburb indistinguishable from new white suburbs in Cape Town, Johannesburg or Los Angeles. The most striking house, which stood only a hundred yards from a shack, has large white stucco walls and a Spanish red clay-tile

6

roof.

The offices of the beleaguered coloured 'parliament' lies on what was once the camp's eastern boundary — its large orange assembly hall set more than a hundred yards from the road. The campus of the coloured University of the Western Cape is up the road. Despite its attractive, red-brick dormitories, laboratories and classrooms, and the well-maintained playing fields and tennis courts, the students disdained their 'bush' college. Cynical towards this benevolent expression of white rule, they thought it fitting that squatters ringed their campus.

Fifteen thousand people stayed behind the rugby field in a shanty town called Unibel, named for a nearby industrial area. Another five thousand were up the railroad tracks at a place called Werkgenot (work is pleasure) which overlooked a fetid pond.

MODDERDAM

The brazenness with which the squatters had upset the careful regimentation of housing in Cape Town helped give the camp the feel of a liberated zone. At the front, along Modderdam Road, nothing separated the shanties from passing traffic. The main entrance into the camp was marked by a log next to the curb, which made it easier for cars and pick-up trucks to get over the bump. After crossing a cracked sidewalk, vehicles went down onto a sand path which cut a semi-circle through the settlement. The path, it sometimes seemed, worried white officials more than the presence of the shanty town itself. The Secretary for Bantu Administration, Wilhelm Cruywagen, charged that the path had been so well built that white liberals must have assisted the squatters in its planning and construction.

The path, however, was only the most visible part of the structure and order of the camp. Most of the coloureds, who comprised about ten percent of Modderdam's population, lived closest to the road. No one had told them to build their shacks together nor did they know each other before arriving at the camp. A 'natural apartheid', as one observer described it, divided the Afrikaans-speaking coloureds and the Xhosa-speaking Africans.

Within yards of each other in this part of the camp stood the best and worst homes I visited at Modderdam. Mrs Abrams lived

7

with her nine-year-old son in a solid A-frame which her brother, a carpenter, had built for her. She had one room furnished with a rocking chair, a chest with glass doors, and a bed covered neatly by a red and white quilt.

Mr Verster's crumbling shack swarmed with flies and stank of old cooked food and shit. Pots and pans were scattered on the dirt floor. Mr Verster, whose four front teeth were out and whose faced was caved in, sat for hours on the bed with his skinny wife whose dry stringy hair hung over her eyes. Their baby sat quietly on the floor, her belly swollen from malnutrition.

The best organized section of Modderdam lay near its centre. Many older residents lived there, including single women who helped staff a soup kitchen and prepare for the weekly clinic. The paths between the houses were usually free of garbage and the refuse pits were carefully soaked with disinfectant. There were tiny gardens of mealies, squash, string beans and carrots. One woman had even grown marigolds which she protected with chicken wire.

A poorer, less cohesive group of neighbours lived off to the right. Shacks here were bunched even closer than in the rest of the camp. Sometimes one wall was used in common for two shanties. Tin roofs which elsewhere were nailed to cross-beams here were held down simply by rocks and broken bricks. Residents quarrelled constantly over the representatives they had chosen to speak for them in the executive committee of the camp. Washing, cooking, and other chores were often done communally at Modderdam, but in this section most families fended for themselves.

People of the camp called the area furthest from the road 'uncivilized'. There were still bushes around the shanties, many of which were made only of plastic and cardboard. They were at the bottom of a slope, difficult to see or reach. White officials usually did not bother to visit them. After December, 1976, when all construction was stopped by the government, new structures would often be thrown together there during the weekends.

It was often said to be the haunt of thieves. I was told that a man who had raped one of the young girls of the camp had lived in one of those shacks. Three men caught him one night while a fourth went to get the police. The suspect was dragged to a blue tent which social work students had erected, but the man tore a hole in the cloth and disappeared. He returned the next night, took his belongings, and left Modderdam.

ORDER

Because most of the squatters were in transition from the country to the city, the community of Modderdam was a strange blend of a working-class town and an African village.

Life at Modderdam usually moved to a rhythm common to poor people. Weekdays, most men worked and women who did not wash, cook or clean for whites did their own housekeeping or visited the hospital. Saturdays were for drinking and shopping. Some of the men went off to the racetrack at Milnerton, a few miles away. Sundays were for church, the community meeting and visiting.

The train to town stopped a mile up the tracks across from the Werkgenot squatter camp. At six or earlier, residents could be seen walking to the station or lining up for the bus. The few men who remained in the camp were either nightwatchmen, casual workers, · self-employed, unemployed or pensioners. Casuals were often men who had no rights to work in the city and depended on odd jobs from employers anxious for cheap labour who ignored the government's labour laws. Most of the unemployed had come from rural areas on contracts which had either expired or been cancelled. The most ambitious men at Modderdam were those who had set up shops or had invested in old pick-up trucks which they used as taxis and to bring in water, food and fuel to sell in the camp.

As few women had rights to live or work in the city, most only left the camp for water. It sometimes took the whole day to do the laundry. Water carried from Belhar was poured into two large drums, one for soaking and scrubbing, the other for rinsing. The women would often work together in groups of two or three to the accompaniment of a record player powered by a large dry cell battery. They had only a few discs, however, and in some parts of the camp the same African tunes were played for several hours on end.

The cooking was done over coal or wood fires or on paraffin stoves. The staple food was *mpoqoshu*, a mash of mealie-meal and beans. Few of the residents could afford any meat other than offal

— the kidneys, intestines, stomachs and other organs which were either boiled or cooked over open fires.

It is hard to say how many stores there were or even what made up a store. Every third or fourth person usually had something to sell, even if it was just some oranges, tomatoes or small tins of instant *Ricoffy*-brand coffee. One man sold only bread while others had whole shacks filled with cigarettes, mealie-meal, fish oil, washing powder, sugar, tea and sometimes dried, smoked snoek. One woman sold live chickens in instalments of fifty cents over four weeks. They were, she laughed, the 'black man's refrigerators'. 'It is the only way we can keep them fresh until we eat them.'

The meeting place was at the centre of the camp. On Sundays at about 10 a.m., a hundred or more men and women brought benches to the spot and listened to the deliberations of the judicial committee and the news of the executive committee.

'People wherever they may be need laws,' the court prosecutor Mr Kekana explained. 'Without these, life can be miserable and chaotic.' Because the camp was dominated by people from 'up country', the court procedure was similar to that of an African village. In fact, the coloureds and Africans who had grown up in the city knew nothing of how to run a trial or present a case, as they had always lived where there were only white-run courts. The coloureds at times resented being judged by the 'tribal' or 'makgotla' court in which those found guilty were sometimes beaten. In the proceedings, the judicial committee took the place of the tribal elders. The secretary of the committee had a role similar to that of the chief. A resident who had a complaint against one of his or her neighbours would inform one of the committee members that he or she wanted to press charges. Mr Kekana, who had grown up in the family of a chief and knew the ways of the village courts well, would investigate the charge and decide whether there was sufficient reason to take the case and present it at the general meeting. No person was appointed to defend the accused, but men and women in the crowd watching the case were free to voice arguments or objections, all of which had to be answered before the committee passed judgement.

A village chief has the authority to deny a man use of tribal lands. The judicial committee was authorized to charge R10 or R15 depending on the offence. It could also evict a serious offender from Modderdam and dismantle his shack. The sentence was only carried out four or five times — once against a thief and once against a man suspected of being a security police informer. Many of the squatters believed that in the other two or three cases, the charges were due to personal grudges. The court, it was said, was becoming 'arrogant'. No special rules governed when a person who was convicted should be caned. In fact, the committee usually denied to outsiders that the practice took place at all.

Often a person would bring a charge against a man or woman for an insult. One case which took an entire morning to settle was brought by a woman who could not find a dress she had laid down on her bed. She suspected that a woman living a few shacks away had stolen it. Yet in the proceedings it became apparent that she was angry with the woman because she thought her neighbour was stealing her husband. At the trial, the two women spent a long time arguing with each other until the committee searched the two houses. The dress was found in the home of the accused but the court later decided that it had been planted by the woman who had brought the charges.

The meeting would usually last for three or four hours, hampered by a protocol and oratory which many of the residents did not take seriously. Those who had lived in town the longest found it hard to take all the proceedings seriously and often dismissed them as 'village politics'. 'I can't waste my time with their bloody nonsense,' one man said to me one day as we watched the court. 'Let's go. Otherwise we'll be sitting here the *whole* day.'

Many of the members of the judicial committee were also on the executive committee, whose members were nominated from different sections of the camp. The executive committee collected funds for the defence of Modderdam in the white court in Cape Town and led the campaign to save the camp. While the members of the committee looked upon themselves as the spokesmen for the camp, they did not have as much power in the camp as they would have liked. Many families stayed aloof from the organization and hardly knew that it existed. Those in the 'uncivilized' section didn't bother to send a representative to the Sunday meetings. At times, it appeared as if the struggle to unify the camp was as difficult as the struggle against the government.

It was very hard for an outsider to determine the depth of divisions and rivalries within the camp. Many residents who wanted their community to win the support of sympathetic whites denied that there were any splits or factions at all because they wanted Modderdam to be seen as a peaceful, unified camp. As in a village, however, many of the quarrels were over buying and selling. There were constant complaints that the prices were much higher in the shanty town than in the city. The women, particularly, thought this was unfair because they rarely dared to leave the camp.

There was also stiff competition between the merchants who lived in the camp and those from outside who came to peddle their goods. On Saturdays, several pick-up trucks full of firewood, fruit and vegetables drove through the camp, forcing some of the residents to lower their prices. The bitterest rivalry was between the shop-owners who lived in the camp and the few men and women who had homes elsewhere in Cape Town but had built shacks in the camp to use only as shops. Mr Sikonyela, who lived in Langa, owned a chain throughout the shanty towns — one shop at Modderdam, two at Unibel, and a fourth at Crossroads. His prices were cheaper, but he was not liked.

'He is taking all our money out of the camp.'

'He is just here for profit and will be the first to go when we are told to leave.'

At one of the meetings of the executive committee, it was decided that if a person left Modderdam and wanted to sell his shack, no person with a house in the township could buy it.

There were also in the camp the religious differences which exist throughout black South Africa between those who still worship ancestors, visit healers (sangomas) and believe in witchcraft; those who belong to Christian black separatist churches; and those who prayed as Anglicans, Protestants or Catholics.

The people who visited sangomas said that illness, starvation, and other suffering amidst health and prosperity was evidence of witchcraft. They thus believed that the whites who had pushed them off the land and hunted them in the bush were either under evil influences or were possibly witches themselves.

The separatists saw the whites simply as part of a world desecrated by sin, greed, anger and jealousy. Unlike separatists in other parts of Africa who have often led popular rebellions, those in South Africa did not criticize the whites or their laws. They used their faith instead to withdraw for a few hours each week.

A young African man, now a poet, once told me of his past career as a 'prophet' in a separatist church, the Zion Apostolic Church. He said he was a 'Christian sangoma'. 'I had a beautiful white robe with a green sash. I carried a cane with me, which is what gave me my power. On Sundays we would come together at the church and start singing and marching with a drum up a hill about a mile away. As I climbed, I could feel what people around me were thinking or if they had sinned. When we got to the top, there was a small wooden fence we had built. I would preach in front of it, and then we would walk aside. That was our Zion — in that little place, that is where people were safe, where they could be at peace.'

The members of the 'established' churches explained their fight against the government as a Christian struggle, and welcomed and campaigned for the support of anti-government white church groups. A white priest who also served the white churches nearby presided over the Anglicans, who prayed at a little shack called 'St John's'.

The different religions at Modderdam were seldom sharply defined. Many of the residents participated in rituals from all three traditions, and there were those who belonged to the established churches who believed at least in the possibility of witchcraft. Yet to the extent that distinctions could be drawn, a squatter's beliefs and rituals tended to reflect the length of time he or she had spent in the city and his or her education. It was this clash between the newer and older immigrants which often set off quarrels over the administration of the camp and the methods used to defend it.

Yet it was colour which divided the camp most deeply. Several Africans charged that the coloureds felt superior and were not behind them in their fight to keep the camp. Coloureds, in turn, charged that at times they were being excluded from the organization of Modderdam. This mistrust was principally caused by laws which gave coloureds a few privileges. They were allowed to stay in the city and were promised alternative sites nearby if they would leave the camp. If the Africans left, though, the women and children would be sent into 'exile' in the rural areas from which they had come. Thus the Africans were worried that the coloureds would ultimately desert them. 'They are on the same train as we are,' an African said, 'but they will get off a few stops before we do.'

This suspicion, though, was not insurmountable. The coloureds clearly felt closer to the Africans who were of their own class than to the residents of Belhar, many of whom lived as prosperously as whites. The people in Belhar, in turn, seemed at times to have more sympathy for the Africans than for the coloureds who were the people they had left behind as they moved into the middle class. A professor at the University of the Western Cape, collecting funds to support the squatters, was told by one woman, 'I will give for the Africans, but not for those *slapgat* (flabby-assed) coloureds.' Throughout the campaign to save the camp, the squatter leaders tried to use the economic conditions which drew the groups together in order to overcome the legal privileges which set them apart.

2. Men

The incongruity of Modderdam's setting was matched by the paradox of the men's life in the camp. Most worked under white employers by day and defied white officials by night — a resistance in part made possible by sympathetic white lawyers, community workers and students. The squatters were thus suspicious of all white intentions but were also able to appreciate and sometimes laugh at the contradictions in their struggle.

Two months before the demolition began, a white-run squatter assistance organization opened an office at Kenilworth Centre, a shopping mall which houses a RAVE supermarket, a record shop, a hardware store, a few restaurants and several clothes boutiques. Both squatters and the liberal beau-monde were invited to a wine and cheese party to view the stark photographs of the squatter camps which lined the office walls.

Several husbands and wives from Modderdam were asked to come, but the men arrived alone in rough pants, old jackets and soiled ties and quickly descended on the food table, working their way through the jugs of Tassenberg red and Bergkeller white. One man wandered over to speak with the women who had sponsored the evening and kept himself standing by tugging on the sleeves of their dresses. When the guests began to disperse, the men began to fill their pockets with the leftover cheese and ornate loaves of bread supplied by a bakery. As they made their way down the stairs to the van they had borrowed for the night, two women chased after them demanding back the bread. They ordered them to return to the office and empty their pockets. The squatters, who had not had so much fun in a long time, obliged courteously.

I saw the men of Modderdam at camp meetings, at protest demonstrations, and in angry skirmishes with the police, but it is this incident, through its humour, which suggests their character most vividly. It was a group that was out of place in the city but neither self-conscious nor in awe of the wealth which surrounded it.

TWO LEADERS

I came to know Mr. Simon Plaatjie and Mr. Winston Matthews better than the other residents of Modderdam. They worked as organizers in the camp, partially supported by donations from other squatters and from an outside community group. Each morning the two men worked through the newspapers to find out what was being said about the camp and waited to see which of the authorities would arrive to inspect the camp and which community workers would come to give them aid. The two men also walked the grounds to listen to complaints and suggestions and to make sure each family dumped its garbage into refuse pits, cleaned the toilets and soaked them with disinfectants.

Mr. Plaatjie was a stocky man with a round face and a dark black skin. He stuttered slightly and was often silent and withdrawn. His wife Mavis was tall and broad. She was as loud as he was quiet. She liked to shout at the officials who patrolled the camp, whereas her husband attempted to ignore them. Nona, their six-year-old daughter, was well-behaved and liked to help her mother with chores. Welcome, the nine-year-old son, spent much of his time playing a form of 'king-of-the-hill' on the small sand dunes in the camp.

The Plaatjies had moved to Modderdam in July, 1976, because the noise and quarrels in Mrs. Plaatjies' parents' four-roomed house had become unbearable. Eight adults and five children were sleeping there.

The house at Modderdam was built in five days. Mr. Plaatjie had bought zincs, wooden poles, and used lumber from a scrap yard for R100, rented a truck from a friend for R5, and arrived at the camp on a Saturday morning. He sank the posts into foot-deep holes, joined them at the sides with wooden slats and attached cross beams for the roof. The frame was finished by evening. He hammered on the zincs the next day, overlapping each sheet by a few inches. He saved the newest pieces for the roof. The floor was laid and the door hinged on Monday and Tuesday. The family moved in on Wednesday.

Upon entering Modderdam by the main path, one saw the Plaatjies' house first on the left. It was painted white with a red window frame and had a yard. Mr. Plaatjie had knocked sticks of bamboo into the ground, stretched wire between them and marked off an area of about twenty feet surrounding the house. He had separated stand from stand on land he did not own in order to set his shanty apart.

Everyone knew Mr. Plaatjie's place, 'the one with the yard'.

Three stepping stones and a place mat led to the Plaatjie's door. Nona was always brushing them clean as there were many guests. Inside there were three rooms each about eight feet square, and a smaller storeroom.

The kitchen furniture consisted of a long wooden table which stood to the right of the outside door. Plastic bowls, a few pans, a long knife, wooden spoons, and a large soup pot were usually stacked on one half. A small brass paraffin burner called a 'primus stove' was placed next to the utensils. A rod used to increase the pressure to burn the fuel extended out of the base of the 'primus'. It was a bit of an art to pump the rod fast enough, hold the basin still, and light the match to get the flame.

A door at the back of the kitchen led to the bedroom which was large enough for a few folding chairs, a wooden three-legged chest propped up by a stack of books and a metal-frame bunk bed. Mr. and Mrs. Plaatjie slept on the bottom, two of the children on top. Mrs. Plaatjie also used the room for the knitting and gossip circles which gathered in her house several afternoons a week.

The storeroom which stood to the left of the kitchen was cluttered with old clothes, used tins of paraffin, a broken table and old newspapers. A clothes line hung a few feet from the roof. The wall between the storeroom and the sitting-room had a hole cut in the shape of a church window. Mr. Plaatjie had spent much time curving the arches with a dull saw.

A pink muslin curtain in the sitting room covered the hole. The walls were prepared with long strips of magazine covers of the December 8, 1976 edition of *Darling*. A brunette with blue eye shadow was the cover girl. 'Is living together a lousy idea?' and 'How to look great when you go out tonight' were the feature articles.

The room was crowded with a puffy orange couch, two chairs, a coffee table, and a stand-up radio. It was a comfortable place in which to drink the tea with sweetened condensed milk that Mrs. Plaatjie served in glass cups. I once sat on the couch, reading a newspaper, listening to a Mozart flute quartet over the English service of the South African Broadcasting Corporation and felt strangely at home in the shanty town.

For the Plaatjies, Modderdam soon became home. They made friends quickly. They liked the independent spirit of the camp, so different from that of the well-patrolled townships. Mr. Plaatjies' favourite place in the camp was also his son's, the top of the dune behind his house. From there it was possible to see the whole camp. I often arrived at Modderdam and found him standing at the edge, his black knitted cap pulled over his ears, his arms folded, just watching.

Mr. Matthews was a small bony man with a bad back who laughed a lot, drank too much, and told flamboyant stories of his life as a squatter. He was sixty. Mr. Plaatjie, who was thirty-five, called him 'Daddy'. Mr. Matthews called himself 'the squatter king', the 'bush president', and once, 'the prime minister of pondokkie-land.' He liked to wear a caved-in grey hat, a narrow black tie and suspenders. He had lived in shanty towns around Cape Town since the early forties.

In each one, he tried to organize the residents to prevent quarrels within the camp and to protect the residents from the government and from 'skollies' (hoodlums). Without some rule in a camp, he said, there can be no peace. He had once been in a sprawling town of over twenty thousand people which had had no organization at all. 'That was the worst. Every weekend you would hear of another murder, another shack being burned.'

Mr. Matthews had grown up in a four-roomed railway cottage in Touws River in the Northwestern Cape. His father was a 'coloured' preacher and railway worker. His mother was African, the daughter of a Xhosa chief. Mr. Matthews had attended school and church as a child, and was part of a small group of blacks who, at that time, were given a full English missionary education. A young Scottish woman had even taught him to play the church's small pump organ which had been sent by train from Cape Town.

As a young man during the 1930's, Mr. Matthews had studied at Wilberforce Academy outside Johannesburg, a seminary established by black American missionaries of the African Methodist Episcopal Church, whose headquarters were, and still are, in Harlem. 'I joined AME because at that time, it was the only place where a black man could rise to the top,' he said. Once ordained, he was sent to preach in the shanty towns of Cape Town at a place called Retreat. His parsonage was a six-roomed shanty. 'The walls were fresh zincs. It was the finest house I ever had.'

But Mr. Matthews, who had a wife and six children, could not support his family as a preacher. His wages depended on voluntary contributions, and after a few years of struggling, he went to work on docks, farms, brickfields, factories, and even in the offices of the Department of Native Affairs. Most of his family had since returned to Touws River. His wife had died a few years earlier. At Modderdam an older woman, Mrs. Menge, now cooked and cleaned for him.

In our conversations, Mr. Matthews was always evasive about his political career. His mentor, he said, had been an old African squatter at Retreat who had belonged to the African National Congress, the liberation movement which was founded in 1912, outlawed in 1960, and now based in Lusaka and London. Mr. Matthews himself denied ever having been a member of the organization but there were rumours that he had once spent time on Robben Island, the political prison seven miles offshore in Table Bay. He did, however, admit to having known two of the most respected political leaders in southern Africa. His mother was in the same royal lineage as Nelson Mandela, president of the ANC, who is now serving a life sentence on 'the Island'. Mr. Matthews had also once been friendly with Ntsu Mokhehle of Lesotho who had been educated in South Africa and is now living in exile after being persecuted by the dictator Leabua Jonathan.

Mr. Matthews had led a squatter movement at Retreat during the 1950's. The land he and other shanty dwellers had been occupying was owned either by the squatters themselves or by other blacks who rented out their backyards. The government had proclaimed the area 'white'. It had bought the land as the initial step in the removal, and informed the squatters that until the homes were knocked down, they would have to pay rent to the government.

Many of the residents had been on the site for several years and had been able to expand and fortify their shacks until they were almost as comfortable as homes with more solid foundations. They refused to give the buildings to the government. After listening to the residents complain for several weeks, Mr. Matthews enlisted the help of three women in the camp. They sent around the word, 'If you own your shack, just break it down and follow us.'

'We decided to take the law into our own hands,' Mr. Matthews grinned. 'We knew we would have to do it over the weekend so that we would already be in the shacks when the superintendent came to work on Monday. I started, and a few others joined in. We mapped out our own plots and said, "Here, you build on this spot. You, you build next to him." More and more people followed and we worked right through the night. We finished in time and some of the men decided to stay home from work to see what would happen. It was really quite funny. We had erected the shacks only a few yards from the superintendent's office. When he arrived he just started yelling at us to demolish the shacks immediately. We told him, "No, that we won't do." '

After two tense days of threats and refusals, Mr. Matthews decided to look for help in Parliament. Mrs. Margaret Ballinger, a white liberal, was then the representative for Africans to the all-white House of Assembly. 'I gathered up a few of the old chaps who knew the whole history of the place, and we went straight in to those beautiful buildings.' After listening for a short while, Mrs. Ballinger agreed to help. The squatters won. The land was proclaimed an emergency camp.

Mr. Plaatjie was not a revolutionary who wanted to fight for Modderdam as part of a struggle for black liberation throughout South Africa. Although he said he 'knew the white man', he knew little political rhetoric. He was driven more by his affection for the community, his pride in his house and his desire to keep the families of his friends together.

Mr. Matthews *did* see the camp's defiance as part of a larger effort to win land and other rights in the city. He did not, however, see it as the beginning of a campaign but as his last battle in a war in which he was becoming too old to participate.

I came to know these two men better than other squatters. I initially thought that they had become leaders because both were sons of a 'coloured' mother and an African father and had grown up at a time when there were few laws separating the two groups. They were, it seemed, in a good position to unify the camp.

Yet as the plight of the camp became increasingly desperate, their background worked against them. Although they spoke

Xhosa fluently, the two men were registered as 'coloureds'. They therefore did not have to carry passes, nor did they risk deportation from the Western Cape. This led some of the Africans in the camp to suspect that Mr. Plaatjie and Mr. Matthews would sell out before the end.

HOSTELS

The central experience which distinguished most of the men at Modderdam from Mr. Matthews and Mr. Plaatjie was hostel life. Those Africans who had come from up country had all spent time in these single-sex dormitories and were, to varying degrees, in rebellion against the living conditions and values of the migrants.

My first impressions of the hostels came through a dry, clinical report on single housing in Cape Town prepared by David Selvan of the University of Cape Town.[1] In his research, he found 'temporary sheds, which were simply large, draughty rooms. In order to conserve heat and obtain some privacy, the forty men living in each room had built shanties of plastic and cardboard *inside* the building.' A large number of the dormitories did not have stoves. Many of those which did were broken. 'The floors are made of cement and none has rubber covering. Only six have any form of covering between the beds.' Selvan also found that the roofs leaked, and because there were neither water drains or gutters, it was impossible to keep out mud and water. There were no kitchens or bathrooms in the buildings.

I later visited one of the better hostels in Langa. There were only two men to a room. The room I saw was smaller than several of the shacks at Modderdam, although in other respects it was more comfortable. There was electricity, a tap just outside the door, and solid brick walls. Inside there was enough space for two beds, a table, a chair, and a small bookcase. The room, though, had only one small window and when the door could not be left open, mildew made the room much more oppressive than many of the shacks at Modderdam.

But I learned most about migrant life during a visit with a friend from Langa to the fifty-year-old 'barracks' in Langa. The weather was clammy. It had rained earlier and children were playing in big puddles in front of four long one-storey buildings which intersected in a cross. A bottle store and a beerhall were burned out in the centre. When we entered a room, it took several minutes before I could make out all the figures because of the dim light and the thick cooking smoke. Two pots were on primus stoves. The filth deadened all colour. A shirt which was once pink was on a hanger opposite a top bunk. The curved end had been straightened into a hole in the plaster wall. The wall itself was pale green and heavy with mildew. Blankets and clothes were thrown together at the foot of many bunks. The smell was like that which clings to clothes, pots and pans during long camping trips. The barracks reminded me of pictures I had seen of mine compounds fifty and sixty years ago. There were about fifteen men inside. A few were sleeping, others were talking in groups, two were washing themselves in a yellow plastic basin with water from an outside tap. There was the clatter of chores and the noise from several conversations, but all sounds were muffled by the dense air of the room.

We sat down with four men. One had lived in the same bunk for over twenty years. Two had been there for ten years. Another had arrived only a short time before. 'We are all from the same village. If someone wants to find one of us, they do not have to give the room number. They just say, "the men from so-and-so."

'Each man buys food for himself and then shares it with his friends. One of the men who has been here for many years is the head. If there are any fights, we go to him.'

A large woman with a wicker basket entered and walked around the bunks shouting 'laundry' in Xhosa. After she had left, a man by the door stood up and asked for silence. He said that he had just received the news that the father of one of the men in the hostel had died up country. Tears ran down his face. Everyone bowed his head and the room was quiet. After a few minutes, the man spoke of his sorrow and of God who gives life and takes it away. Several other men from different parts of the room cried. Finally there was a prayer and the men were told that a collection would be made to send to the family.

The older man sitting opposite me excused himself and returned a few minutes later with a shallow tin bowl of meat which he passed around the circle. After a few minutes he spoke:

'I am from the Transkei. It is there where I was born, there where I chose my wife, and there where I will return when I finish my work here in Cape Town.

'I come from a family that was once wealthy. We had cattle and sheep and fields of corn. As a boy, I herded the cattle, walking up and down the hills near our home, and it was then that I came to love the land.

'But at that time already, men would leave the village for the mines and then come back each year for some months to work in the fields. I remember the big feasts we would have when my father came home. Sometimes he came back leading a cow. Then we would slaughter an ox for a celebration.'

'Now when I was 15 — that must have been in about 1935 — there was a great drought. The crops would not come up and cattle were dying every day. Many more families then decided that the hardships were too great, and the wives and children followed their husbands and fathers to the towns. At that time, it was not hard to do this because the pass laws were not strict. But my father still refused to leave his kraal. "This is our ancestors' land," he said. "It was given to us for now and for all time."

'And so it was to try to save what we had in the village that I first went to the mines. I was at Klerksdorp. We Africans did all the digging and the whites, they were just using their heads. They were the ones always telling you, "go over there, up there, down there."

'Conditions were bad, but we could manage. The food was all right. We had enough beer, even some meat.

'But I did not work long in the mines — only seven years. After that time I wanted to leave because I had seen my friends' backs broken and I myself had been hurt by falling rocks. That was during the war, when there were many jobs and a man did not have to go underground. I decided to come to Cape Town because some of the men from the village had already worked here, and they said the place was all right. I found a job at the docks and came to live here in Langa.

'At the mines, it was easy to keep up with the news from up country, because there were men coming back and forth all the time. But here I discoverd only a few of us Africans. And it was only in these hostels that you could find your homeboys and find out about home. Because almost every week there would be one letter coming from the village and that letter could be read to the whole group.

'Now I had been in Cape Town long when I received word that my father had died. He just went to sleep one morning, and then did not wake up. After that, my goal in life was clear. I was the oldest son, and my father had told me that whatever happened, I

23

must keep the land. And that is what I have struggled to do all these years.'

'At that time, we did not have many heads of cattle left, and my wife could only take care of a small plot of corn. Yet I thought at the time that if I could make enough money, it might be possible to rent a tractor, and that could be the promise of some prosperity. And so I worked hard on the docks, and at times I even took a second job as a nightwatchman. I lived my life in town in only two places — at work and here in the hostel.

'I gradually became used to this place, and it became harder for me to leave it, because I had acquired some responsibility. As I was one of the older men, I was one who helped to keep order in the room, and would also talk to the newer men who came, when it seemed like they were neglecting their families up country, or were causing fights here in the hostel.

'I was not able to save enough money for the tractor, and that still remains a dream — even though I am now becoming old. But I was able to send enough money up country so that my wife could stay up there. Now I am getting help in supporting her, because my two sons are also working in town, and they are sending home some rands as well.

'It was this success in supporting my family up country which led me to feel that I did not want my wife to come down here with me. I needed her there to watch the land. Even now, when times are very hard, I do not want her to leave, because then I would be in danger of losing everything I have worked for all these years. Were she to follow me here, the chief might soon give the land to someone else, and then I would have broken the oath to my father, and I would have no place of security — either here or up country.

'I have sometimes thought that I have made a mistake in my life — and that after I first came home from the mines to marry, I should have brought my family with me. But a man must stick to the choices he has made if he can. Now, after all this time, the only thing I want in this Cape Town is more work, more overtime, and more money. If I am lucky these next few years, I might save enough to buy a new house for when I go home to finish my life.'

LAND ABANDONED

None of the men I met at Modderdam had as close an attachment to the land as did Mr. Phakathi. His commitment to the village was considered old-fashioned and to some extent, harmful, because it could lead whites into thinking that *all* Africans could or wanted to return home.

The man who sympathized most with the hostel-dweller was Mr. Ndiki. He was also a landowner, and this made him slightly jealous of those migrants who were still able to keep their families at home.

'For those of us who still have a homestead, it is difficult when our wives come. For we are feeling that while we want to be with them, we also want them at home to protect what we have there.

'I first came to Langa in 1947. But while I have been there all this time, I have always kept my roots in the country. The life in Cape Town never really attracted me. I could not see how a man could spend his whole life in a house without ever hoping to buy it. At least in the country, I can build if I have money.

'I left my wife in the country all those years until I brought her to join me here in 1975. I had difficulty going to visit the family every year because the time I could be at home varied every year. Often it was only for a few weeks, and that was far from being long enough. But each time I went home, I could see what was happening to the land up country. There were so many diseases which were unheard of before. And there were all kinds of hardships which forced men to their knees and made their wives abandon the country in order to be with their husbands.

'This is what happened to my wife. She had been feeling pains all over her body. She came to hospital in town. At first she received a month's permit. When that expired, she had just begun to feel better and we knew it would be harmful for her if she was to return home. I decided then that after all those years in the hostels, it was safer to come out here to Modderdam because the raids are fierce in the townships, and it costs lots of money to keep women out of police cells.

'So you can see, it is not simply for fun that we came to this camp. It is like something that we have been pushed to do. For if I could receive the same money in the Transkei as I receive here, I would return home. But until such a time, I now think that it is better that I try to stay here at the camp — because I know that the health of my wife is more important than my land. Maybe when I retire, we can go back.'

TWO WIVES

At the other extreme from Mr. Ndiki was Jackson Thubu, 60. When a young man, he also had come to Cape Town to work as a migrant, but he had quickly cut his links with his village. His shock was that now, after all this time, the responsibilities of that village life had caught up with him.

'The big change in life is that young men today believe in staying with their wives. Perhaps this is because they become lovers before they marry. With me, I got to a certain stage in my life when I negotiated with my father about marriage. I just pointed to a girl I thought I would like — she had not even seen me once. Both families agreed, and then that girl became my wife.

'Personally I am not sorry to see these arranged marriages fade. No, I am not sorry. Because it was this, I believe, that was the source of my troubles.

'Immediately after marrying I had to leave for town to work for the lobola cattle. I went to the mines three times. Of course, while men today still go there, most of them do not buy cattle with the money. Rather they just send that money home to try to support the family. I went back and forth to the village as most men did. I had my family there and provided for them.

'But all this changed when I came to Cape Town. It was just after the war and it was easy to find a job in the factories. I went to Paarl (east of Cape Town) and found a place to live in the township. It was easier to do this then because you did not have to worry about a pass.

'After a short time I met a woman there and we decided to live together. I lived with her as a sub-tenant in the house for many years. I did not stay close to my other family. I worked 22 years in one factory, 11 in another. Then last year, a son from my first wife found me in Paarl. He got my address from my brother and came with his mother. There were fights in the house and so I had to separate from the other woman. That is why we came here.'

'And your wife? How was it for her during those years?'

'How she lived, I don't know. She tells me that life was hard and miserable and I believe it was so. But I do not think she bears

26

a grudge against me. For I think she may understand that it is quite a hard thing for a man who is married to stay without a woman whether it is his wife or some other person. In that way, I can say the migrant system is to be blamed. It was like an evil spirit that kept us apart until I no longer had that strong feeling for the family. I do not always believe in witchcraft, but sometimes things happen in front of your eyes and you are just forced to believe that wicked spirits are working against men to make them forget other people. It is a great pity because I have spent all my energy and health away from her and am returning to her at an old age when I can no longer work.'

'Do you have guilt feelings?'

'I can say that I do. Because now my children are grown and I have not helped them. I am not a happy man. But as I look at my son, I see that he may have it worse. At least I enjoyed the security of one job for a long time whereas today a young man must renew his contract every year and sometimes not to the same employer. More money is coming in than when I was young, but there is little a man can do with it. The pass laws and many other laws regulating the Africans in towns seem to make it very difficult to build a house or save for anything. Thus my son is staying here at this camp with much anxiety, for he knows that he can be chased away tomorrow.'

UNEMPLOYED

The majority of the men at the camp were young. They were unable to support their families, able to find work in Cape Town, but unable to bring their families to the city. John Mongo, 28, had recently lost his job. As a migrant without a contract, he found himself with offers of employment yet caught in a legal tangle similar to that of Sizwe Bansi in the play by John Kani, Winston Ntshona and Athol Fugard, *Sizwe Bansi is Dead.* Sizwe, who comes from King William's Town in the Ciskei, is trying to get permission to work in Port Elizabeth. His city-wise friend, Stiles, explains the correct bureaucratic procedure for him to follow:

'You talk to the white man, you see, and ask him to write a letter saying he's got a job for you. You can take that letter from the white man and go back to King William's Town where you show

27

it to the Native Commissioner there.

'The Native Commissioner in King William's Town reads that letter from the white man in Port Elizabeth, who is ready to give you the job. He then writes a letter back to the Native Commissioner in Port Elizabeth. So you come here with the letters. Then the Native Commissioner in Port Elizabeth reads the letter from the Native Commissioner in King William's Town, together with the first letter from the white man who is prepared to give you a job, and he says when he reads the letter, "Ah yes, this man Sizwe Bansi can get a job."

'So the Native Commissioner in Port Elizabeth then writes a letter which you take with the letters from the Native Commissioner in King William's Town and the white man in Port Elizabeth to the Senior Officer at the Labour Bureau, who reads all the letters. Then he will put the right stamp in your book and give you another letter from himself which together with the letters from the white man and the two Native Affairs Commissioners, you take to the Administration Offices here in New Brighton and make an application for a Residence Permit, so that you don't fall victim to raids again. Simple.'[2]

'My story is like that of many other people,' John Mongo said. 'As I grew up there was no necessity for me to work, for my father had livestock. Life was good until he died. Then our cattle dwindled. Some died, and others had to be sold to make money. We also could not afford to rent tractors. So I had to go out and stand up by myself, support my family, and earn money for marriage. These were my aims when I first came to Cape Town — to support my mother and work for lobola.'

'Where did you stay?'

'In the barracks in Langa. There were twenty of us in the room. I had heard many people talk of the hostels, but without seeing them for yourself, you really can't know what happens there. It was very hard at first because in the country, one is more independent. A man can be by himself or be alone with a woman. But in the hostels, there were all kinds of rules. If a woman was caught inside, the man is fined R15 and the woman R20. I learned quickly that if you are going to have a girl-friend in there, you must always keep R35 in your pocket.

'In order to live in peace, we had to organize ourselves. We drew up rules, and if a man did something wrong, we charged fines.

Gradually, I became used to the place.'

'Were you able to save money?'

'It was hard, but a group of us got together and contributed money in rounds. In this way, I was able to send home about R20 a month.

'I married after two years. My wife stayed at home, but I worried because I knew I was not sending enough money. When I came home after the first year, I told her to come back with me. We first went to Elsie's River and then went to a squatter "farm", where we paid a man to let us live on the land. We were living quite peacefully there until last year when the shack burned down. The landlord said he didn't want us putting up a new one, so we had to leave.

'After all this time, we had very little left at home. All my brothers had come to town, and my mother was the only one still staying there. It was then that we decided to come to Modderdam.'

'How did you hear of it?'

'We were just passing by one day and saw people putting up shacks. I asked them who owned the land and they said they didn't know — everyone was just building.'

'Were you still employed?'

'Yes. All the time, I was in a garage. It was a good job, as far as pay. But I worked *very* hard, often seven days a week. I was a watchman. I had no complaints about the salary, but we had no days off, no pensions, or any other benefits. So one day, I and another man went to the *baas* and told him about these things. He said we were talking nonsense and that there were plenty of others who were in need of jobs. He thought we would get others to complain as well and try to strike.

'That day, we were paid our wages for the week and told to go. Of course, when that happened, my pass was no longer right, and I could not get another contract unless I went back to the Ciskei. But I knew that near King William's Town, where I live, the only people who get contracts are those from the cities who have them already and are just there to renew them. One may wait three months or more, and then one is forced to just go to town illegally and try to get casual jobs.

'So I stayed here doing these odd jobs. In good months, I could make as much as I had in my old job. I could usually get work on construction sites because the employers would hire us illegals because we would work for less money. But then they started saying that "coloureds" are supposed to get our jobs and we are supposed to go back where we came from. They check passes at work. So the employers are less willing to hire us because if they are caught, they must pay fines. Now I am just getting by because my brother is helping us out.

'The government here says our chiefs want us at home, but our chiefs say that they can do nothing for us and we are much better off in the city. I am in quite a hopeless position. There is little here for me and my family, but it does not help to take them back to where they starve. Under these circumstances, we black people are forced to be stubborn.'

'Do you think things will change?'

'I don't know. But I feel these hardships burning inside me, in my heart. I know that when you talk this way, you may land on Robben Island. But a coward must become brave one day.'

3. Women

In speaking of their lost lands, their abandoned hostels and their jobs, the men of Modderdam told how they and their people were forced from their villages yet denied life in the city. The women of the camp told the other side of this story. In the rural areas they had once been farmers, but now they only waited for the mail. In the cities, they had once been allowed to live in houses but now they were chased like animals in the bush.

Like the men, there were those women who hoped to return to their villages some day and those who saw such a life as banishment. Yet despite the differences in their education and their attachment to the land, the women often spoke of how their struggle drew them together to generate a 'strong spirit' and a 'good feeling'.

At a meeting with a group who had gathered in a large shack, one woman explained, 'Here we often have a greater chance to make friends than in the country. Up there, most of the people you visit are relatives whom you have known your whole life. This can be quite boring. Here people make friends with those who happen to live next to them. Occasionally you might know some of the people from the village or from another squatter camp, but usually you make friends with people you have never seen before.

'We have some of the fights you might find elsewhere. Yet we find usually that there is good cooperation for we all know each other's condition and we all need the same things. When one of us is sick or has to bring children to hospital, usually we help out and take over her chores. When we get together to do the washing or cooking or just to talk, we usually discuss buying food, or the chances of getting a job outside, or personal problems with our children or our husbands.

'What brings us together the most, though, is our desire to stay here. Many of us, especially those from the country, feel that we would rather live in a place like Modderdam than in one of the townships. Life would be harder if all of the new people were just scattered around. What matters to us is not so much the condition of our houses, but the help you get from people around you. You might think that people would only make friends with those who are most like them — that is how it often is in the townships. But here we find it is not so. There are some young village girls who have got to know the older ones from the town quite well. They teach them about this Cape Town.'

A SURVIVOR

The oldest woman I met at Modderdam was Mrs. Siyosana Mpendu. She was short with a leathery face. All but two of her front teeth had fallen out. She spent her day hunched on a bench in front of her home smoking a foot-long wooden pipe which rural Xhosa women smoke. As if to parody her new life in the town, she wore a traditional Xhosa turban around her head and pink sneakers on her feet.

Her link to her village was stronger than that of any other woman I interviewed at the camp. Yet while she talked about going home 'in a few days', she was there for months, and her neighbours doubted whether she would leave while the shack in which she was staying was still standing.

She was respectful towards whites, and would in no way regard herself as a rebel. But in her understanding of how white men and their technology had destroyed Xhosa culture, she revealed a political awareness which was both bitter and comic.

'I do not know how old I am, but I can tell you what happened in those times. When the black fever swept our country, I was as old as that young girl there.' She pointed to a girl with tightly knitted hair who looked about fifteen. The 'black fever' was the flu epidemic which swept the world in 1918.

'People were dying everywhere. In one family, maybe only one person was left. We were burying people every day. At that time, it was a rare event for the men to go to work in town. We just used to plough the fields. I worked very hard every day. We didn't even use oxen then. Just a hoe and our hands. But it was not so bad for us because we were used to it. The women now cannot work like us. We were much stronger.'

'Did you ever see white people?'

'Hardly ever. And to see a car was a very rare thing too. People used to go to the Transvaal on foot, and catch a train from Dordrecht. We had to prepare a lot of samp for the men when they left. They would go to the mines and come back driving a cow. In those days, men would go to the towns for six months then come back and stay for maybe a year. They would only go back when they needed money. There was no Cape Town for us in those days, only Johannesburg.

'When the men came back from the mines, sometimes you would hear of men who had been hurt or killed there. But we women did not hear many of those stories because husbands don't tell their wives such things. But all those years that my husband went away, I never wanted to go with him.'

'Why not?'

'In those days, it was not so important for the men and women to be together here, because the men would come home for some time. But now because of the problems men experience in coming to town they neglect their families and place more importance on their work. And so it becomes necessary for the women to come. My husband when he went to the mines used to send us lots of money. Now some of the men send, but others do not. I don't know what they do with all the money in the towns. But I think they use it for liquor. This too is new. My husband died without ever touching the bottle.'

'Do you still farm?'

'No. I am old now. But I have my land although it is now so poor and dry. People used to start ploughing the land in October. Never in December as they do now. In those times, a boy like that one over there would know no hardships.'

She pointed to a young man who said he was seventeen.

'There was plenty of food. There was a lot of milk — one cow would give us enough for a whole family. Now even if you have a whole herd, there is often little to drink.'

I asked her when conditions deteriorated.

'I cannot tell you the exact year, because I am not educated. But now our children are having problems because they are getting milk from the white people.'

The audience which had begun to form while she spoke laughed. She laughed as well, then explained.

'Whites feed their children for about three days and then they give them something like a purgative. But with us, we do not get this medicine and the children become constipated. And now they have these other foods like Nestum from the white people and they also cause problems. Though in the advertisements you see a healthy baby, it is not.'

More laughter. Nestum is a baby food sold in jars.

The conversation stalled and I asked her if she liked Modderdam.

'This is a funny place. What do I have to do here? People spend too much money on bread and oranges. At home we have dry porridge, sour milk and samp only.

'And the town is very corrupt. I remember my very brother who grew up as a straight-forward person, upright and with good habits. I noticed as time went on that he was increasingly developing loose habits, smoking and drinking excessively and gradually neglecting his family down here. He had five children. His family was starving in a way I cannot tell. But previously he had been a man who loved his wife and children. The town spoiled a good person and I know many others who have lost their good personalities as a result of the influence of the town. We discovered that in fact he had been staying with a widow here in Cape Town. All his money was used up in that house buying furniture and maintaining the children he had with her. The town women have wigs and bright complexions and dress smartly to attract our men and we who are in the country are forgotten. His wife is now like a mad person. His children are all scattered. The woman he used to stay with threw him out when he could no longer work. He lived for drinking every day. He lost respect for his own children and there is nothing he can do for himself. Women in town are to blame for taking our men away but I think now that if a woman came with her husband to this Cape Town, she would not lose him easily.'

'Would you like to stay here forever?'

'No. Here you cannot have anything of your own except cars. I am just staying in this place with my children until the doctors tell me I can go back. I have pains in my chest. This too is new. Because before we never had to come to the doctors in the towns because our own were quite good — they were much more powerful than they are today. They used to heal all sick people and would work out their own cures. When a young one was sick, they did not sleep but worked all night with their own medicines.'

'Do you mean sangomas?'

'Yes. I myself am one. I learned as a girl, after I became ill. When I got better, they slaughtered a goat and made some beer and poured in some medicines. I was given it to eat and then my ancestors came into contact with me and taught me many things. I worked on people who have pains in their body, and things like that. I never use bones — just touch people with my hands.'

I asked her to speak more of witchcraft and healing but she said no, she was tired, and we asked too many questions. As we thanked her, she said, 'If I look at my life and the others around here, I say again that the greatest problem now is that the men are married to the city, not to their wives. When my husband began working in Johannesburg he did not have a pass, but by the time he stopped he had one and hardly ever came home. That is why I call this place a land of suffering.'

THREE COMMUTERS

Mrs. Mpendu was one of the only African women in the camp who expected to return to her village to live out her life. Most of the others were determined to spend their days in the city, although some found themselves pulled back and forth between the two places.

Mrs. Esther Dywile was the only woman I met whose husband had two wives. She was shy and at first adopted the style of response black people learn quickly when asked questions by whites — her shoulders hunched, her eyes looking down at the floor as she spoke. To put her more at ease, my interpreter spoke to her without interrupting to translate.

'We are happy together to be his wives. But when I was up there with her and my husband was here alone, he sent us different amounts of money, even though we each had two children and were cooking out of the same pot. But when he fails to send us money, there is nothing we can do and as a result we starve.

'I first came here because I fell ill. My husband wrote a letter that I should come and join him to get help. He had already built a shack in this place when I came to join him. I have been here for some time, but my intention is still to return when I have recovered. But I see now that if I do go home, the other wife must come and take my place here in order to look out for our interests. Now, when I am here, I make sure she is sent enough money and I would expect her to do the same for me.

'If my husband could earn the same amount of money in the Ciskei I would happily go back there as I am missing the place every day. At home together, you can plan about building your own house and such things but here there are no prospects of ever owning one. But if he earned less, I would rather tolerate life here because without enough money there is no happiness. I am feeling that it is a cruel thing that white people want to use the labour of our husbands but they have no respect for us as wives.'

Mrs. Twala's visits to her village, Udidi, were taking place at greater and greater intervals. Gradually her link to her village was becoming only a vague desire to return at the end of her life. She was a proud woman who kept her two-roomed shack clean and neat.

'Before my husband and I married we knew each other well and we used to discuss marriage quite deeply and at length during this time. We were married in a Presbyterian church in the country. We knew at the time that my husband would have to go to town to work but we felt that this would be hard as we already had one child and I was pregnant with another. For we wanted to be able to make decisions about our family and our home together. To me, nothing is more important than that there should be some understanding between husband and wife.'

'Did he come straight to Cape Town?'

'Yes. He was on contract and stayed in the bachelors' quarters. He sent me money but it was not enough to pay for food, clothing and medicine. I am convinced that he sent us little money not out of any ill-will towards us, but because he earned fifty rand a month at first and he had to send some money to his mother as well. After some months like this I did not need anyone to tell me what I had to do. I wrote to my husband to tell him that I wanted to join him here and he said that I should, although he told me that it would be difficult as I was not allowed here.'

'Did you take your whole family?'

'I left my eldest son with my mother-in-law and I took the other with me on the bus from Umtata. There were other women who were also coming to join their husbands. I did not take many things with me as I did not know when I might have to go back. When I arrived, it was not too hard to find my husband because I had his address in Langa. He told me that he had been able to build a shack for us at KTC (a camp near the township of Nyanga). We stayed there for some months until I became pregnant. Then it was necessary to move as I needed some privacy and there were others staying in the shack as well. We found a room in a house in Guguletu. But after a time the people with whom we were staying became worried because they feared that if I was discovered, they might lose their house. This was four years ago.

'My husband then decided to move back to the bachelors' quarters and for a time my two children stayed with him until we could decide what to do. Finally we decided that I should go back to the country. So for the next three years I would spend some of the time with my in-laws and then come back down here for a while when the hardships became too great. Then in 1976 my husband said we might be able to build out here. He had heard that many people were already here and that the police were not arresting people so much. I did not like the idea of going just under the bushes, but I thought that I might be able to run a household with my husband, if only temporarily.'

'Do you think wives have a responsibility to take care of the family and land there?'

'Yes, if it can be done. But as my husband has no land to plough and little hope of securing some, this does not have much meaning. And at the same time, it is against the marriage contract for a husband to be taken away from a wife for whatever reason. For when we married we vowed to stay together until our deaths and to build a home together. Yet one sees that when the two are separated there may even be a divorce. Then both parties fall short of the vows they made in church.'

'How long would you like to stay?'

'If it were possible, I would like to be here until my husband became too old to work and we would leave together to stay in the country and live on pension and some savings. But until that time I will not go back there to live unless I am just pushed back.'

Mrs. Ruth Giacala, 35, had become even more settled in the city. As she had moved back and forth between Cape Town and the Transkei, her old faith in her village beliefs had been shattered.

'I no longer believe that if one stays up country, the ancestors there will protect the family, because if that were so, I would not have lost my first child. In fact I am thinking that while I am here in Cape Town I should have as many children as my fertility will allow, for I do not know when I might have to go back and I do not know how many I might lose again at home.

'I can say, too, that unlike my mother, I am more attached to my husband than to my home. When he goes up, I too want to go up. When he goes down, I too want to go down. My mother, she stayed in the country always, but then she saw richer days in the village. Then it was easier to bear children and they had more to eat.

'At first I thought my life would be like hers. I stayed in the country because my husband said I should and because that is what most women did. But in the country I could not conceive because my husband would be home only for a few weeks. Yet when I was born, my father stayed home for some months. So I could say that my mother had a better life than I have.

'After one Christmas I told my husband that I was worried that I might go another year without a child and he suggested that I come down here. It was the first time I had left the country. It was when I arrived that I learned I could be arrested. For a year we lived as sub-tenants in a house in Guguletu. I became pregnant. I was happy because I had got what I wanted — a child.

'Yet after the year, I was missing the country very badly so I took my baby and went back to Umtata. I lived with my in-laws there and when my husband came home the next year, I became pregnant for the second time. Life was hard, but I thought I would stay at home. But then my first child died. The way he cried I thought he had swallowed some poison. I did not want to lose the other child so my husband's parents suggested that I come back down to Cape Town to stay. I wrote to my husband and he agreed. When I arrived the second time he had already prepared and built this shack at Modderdam so we moved in after only a few days. I think I made the right decision because since I have been here, I have been getting more attention and better food and my child's health is good. And after this time, I do not miss the country that much.

'In my mother's time, it was considered a good thing if a woman stayed up country. But now this has changed. I sometimes think that it is a wife's responsibility to come to town. The more women who come the better. For however strong a man may be, he can easily be tempted by another woman. It is no longer judged to be a wrong thing if this happens. However, if the flow of women from the Transkei grows, this practice may come to an end. For we know our husbands respect us more than the city girls because they have paid lobola to have us, unlike those they just live with here.

'I am also thinking that it is our responsibility to come down here for when we see our husbands every twelve or every twenty-four months, our children grow up without knowing the face of their father. There are even times when wives say goodbye to their men when they first leave to seek work and then never see them again. But they are not dead, our husbands. They are living in these Cape Town sands.'

AN IMMIGRANT

For Mrs. Victoria Goloza, 34, the transition from village to town would have been complete, had it not been for the laws keeping her from fully settling in the city.

'I was only thirteen when I married. It was even before my breasts had developed. In fact they only began to grow larger after I had already conceived. I married so young because with the Africans one used to marry as soon as the lobola cattle were offered. The girl must just go. I am not even sure when I had my first child — my husband knows better. I didn't even know what was happening when I was told I was to have a child. The thing is that when one is invited to marry, it is a bad sign for the parents to refuse. The girl may lose her chance. But nowadays, I don't think that a girl should marry so young.

'When I was four months pregnant, my husband left me for the first time to work. He only returned three years later. They were bitter times — my pillow would become wet with tears. I stayed in the village with his family and the most important thing was that I was aware that I was becoming a woman.'

'Why was he away so long?'

'I never discovered why. But he was young as well and perhaps he was becoming a man in a different way in the towns. I did not ask him where he had been when he did not come back for we respect our men and do not ask them such things. But after that, he would send money regularly and come back every year or two.

'In the Transkei I gave birth to nine children. But at about the age of three years, many of these died. After a few of these deaths, I decided to join the church because I thought that God might be able to help me. I used to dream about the church — that I was sitting inside, holding a Bible with my children. I went to the Catholics because as far as I could see, it was the one for poor people like myself. There were not many Catholics in the village but the white sister there was very kind and tried to help me. She would come to the village and teach two of my children to read. I am sorry that I never learned, but I believe that I still could, even now. I have always thought that if I could get enough education and some money, I would like to learn tailoring.'

'How long did you stay up country?'

'For many years. According to tradition, I stayed at my brother-in-law's homestead and we had land on which to build and plough. Yet these days one must hire a tractor to till the land and we did not have enough. My husband could never send enough money home, and thus when my brother-in-law died, conditions became intolerable. When my husband came home on leave, I asked him if I could go back with him. He saw how hard it was for the children and for myself. I took one child with me and left the other two I was caring for with my relatives.

'We first stayed in the bachelors' quarters in Langa. This was before we had enough money to buy zincs. It was terrible staying with so many people and I was worried about being arrested. I did not want to walk around the township. But after a few weeks I was picked up during the night in the hostel. As my husband works nights, I had to leave the child there alone. I was frightened, as this was the first time something like this had happened to me and I thought I might be sent back to the Transkei without my child.

'But my husband came the next day and paid the fine. Then he borrowed more money, bought some nails and zincs and we went to Elsie's River. As my plan was to try and stay permanently with my husband in Cape Town, I knew that I must try to find work. I was able to find a day job, although the madam told me that they could not help me if I was caught with the wrong pass. I have to leave pretty early in order to get there before the officials start checking.'

'Does your employer know you are living here?'

'Yes. They try to help me when they can. But sometimes I

think I am getting paid poorer wages than if I was here with the proper documents.'

'How long would you like to stay in Cape Town?'

'From my success, I see that I should stay forever, even when my husband is too old to work. I do not want to go back to the country for with the death of my brother-in-law, there is nothing to go back for. Many of my relatives have followed me here and are staying at Crossroads and now all my children are in Cape Town. The only people I miss in the country from time to time are my own parents. Here I do not starve, I do not need to go out and ask for food, paraffin, matches, salt, soap and samp, or to put up with feeding just water to my children. In the country you are always being watched from a distance by neighbours and you tire people by nagging them and borrowing food. Also, as you can see on the bed, there are two shawls which I have knitted. Tomorrow I can sell them, and so in this way too I can use my hands to get money. But in the country, there would be nobody to whom I could sell them. For women who are happy in the country, they should stay there and leave here alone. But for myself, I have learned never to be separate from my husband. Let me ask you this: the white man came from Holland to South Africa with his wife and children. But are they told to send them back?

IN THE BUSH

Like Mrs. Goloza, the majority of the women with whom I spoke had abandoned their hope or desire to return to the rural areas. For them, apartheid was a system which did not force them back to the land but made them live as guerillas, wandering from one squatting site to another as they dodged the police. Mrs. Rita Massey, a tall woman with high cheekbones, had become tough and aggressive through her years in shanty towns. She had already adopted many ways of the city and had lost the subservience towards whites which the newer immigrants showed.

Speaking in English, she said that the women could not explain why they were at Modderdam until they spoke of the 'dompass' (dumb pass). 'I ask you,' she said accusingly, 'when you are up country without your husband, what good is it? Can you sleep with it? Can it feed you? Can it give you children? You look at your picture in it. And you think this thing is just a toy. Whether

41

you have it, or another, or just throw it away, you are just the same person.'

'For seven years my husband had been working on the docks on contract. He would return home for three weeks each year but all the time he was away, I would hear nothing from him. I thought he had taken a woman in the city and had to take care of her. How is a woman supposed to live and feed five children when no money comes in the post? I am from the Transkei. It is a dry place. You can grow very little.

'After struggling all those years, I decided to follow my husband to Cape Town because I love him, but I also knew that my children would live only if I was watching him. I took the bus from Umtata (the largest city in the Transkei) and went to Langa. I was scared because I knew my pass was not right. My husband told me that if I was found we would have to pay fines and I would go to jail.

'My husband said that he would find a place in the bush like other people because there I would be safe and we could live together with the children. I had taken two with me, and left the other up country with my mother.'

'How did he know where to go?'

'We hear about all the places, "Werkgenot", "Kraaifontein", "Crossroads", "Snake Park", "Vrygrond", "Skandaaldorp". '

The Masseys found a place near Tiervlei, east of the city. 'It was all right there. I was safe because there were few squatters at that time and no one bothered you. We were not far from water and while my husband was working, I did the cooking and washing. I could not get work and I was afraid to go out on the main road with my children.

'But then he became sick and was in the hospital for months. I had no money but I knew it would be worse in the Transkei. Then my children and I suffered because we were told that we could not stay in that place any longer because they were going to build something there.'

'Where did you go?'

'I had nowhere and no one to help me so I just stayed there. But one day when I was away they took everything out of the shack and burnt it down.

'Then it was real bad. Sometimes I would take my children and ask to stay in other shacks but there were many times when we just went to sleep under the bushes or just whatever I could find

42

to put over our heads. Sometimes women get boyfriends to help them and put up shacks but I had no boyfriend. Finally some Muslim people gave us zinc and helped to put up a little place. It was as big as the toilets here. We could not sleep in it. We just put our heads inside and the sand was always blowing in, and when it rained there was water.

'Then I was able to get some work charring, although I was still scared when I went into town because of my pass. I slowly built my little house. I got more zincs and put up another room. People helped me and gave me food when they could. But I was not very happy because my husband was still in the hospital and my children were not schooling. But finally he came out and found work.'

'When was this?'

'A short while ago. My husband heard that this was a good place here at Modderdam, so we took down the shack and came here. It is a good place, and when we came it was quite nice. It is just next to the bus. The problem is with water. There is none here in the camp so we must go to Belhar or pay ten cents for twenty litres which is a lot because we use water for cooking and washing.'

I asked Mrs. Massey if, after all her struggles, she was glad she had come to Cape Town. She smiled. 'Yes. Because I am able to put out my hands every Friday for my husband's money. We eat meat sometimes and as you can see my stomach is even getting a little fat. You see too that I can buy a special Ambi (a facial cream) for my complexion. It costs only 25 cents, whereas it is much more expensive up country.'

WITHOUT HUSBANDS

The women without husbands had the most desperate need to stay in Cape Town. Many had lived in the city legally for years until they had been widowed or divorced. Then they had lost the rights to their houses and were told to leave for 'homelands' where they might never have lived before and where they had neither land nor home. Thus threatened, they were among the most determined and articulate residents at Modderdam.

Mrs. Bella Phindi was a large, broad-shouldered market woman. During the months in which I came to know her, her store expanded from a paltry stock of vegetables to a good supply of basic foodstuffs. She started selling at a little table in front of her shack, then gradually converted her living room into a shop with shelves and a counter.

I did not know her well until after the demolition. Then we spoke at length as I tried to help her get back into business. Her English was good.

'My mother brought me to Cape Town from Queenstown (on the edge of the Ciskei) when I was still a girl. We just put up a shack. In those days they left you alone. Women did not have to carry passes and people just didn't care where you stayed. I grew up in a shanty town. I have never been out of them. I have never tasted township life. I never used to worry about living in shacks — they were just the places where poor people lived. Food was cheap. My father was a labourer, my mother charred, and the children went to school.'

'Did you think you would always be in a shanty town?'

'For a long time I thought I would have a house. My life would be like my parents', only it would be easier for me. And for a time it was. I married, my husband worked on the docks, and I charred for a family in Bishopscourt (a wealthy Cape Town suburb). But these times came to an end when we women were told that we must have passes. We were tricked. They said that if we had our "dombook" we would be able to travel all over and that if anything happened to our husbands we would get pensions. So we said "Good!" and we all went down to the offices to have our photos taken.

'Nothing happened for five years. I was told I could stay here because my husband was from Cape Town. But when he died, I went to report it at the Langa Superintendent's office and they told me that now I and my children would have to return to the Ciskei. But I had not been there for many years except on holiday. I was now by myself and I knew that I could not go back because there would be no money. But I am a strong woman and I said to myself that I was going to provide for my family here in Cape Town.

'I had to leave the shack where I had stayed with my husband because they knew me there and the inspectors would come around to check passes. So I bought some new zincs and moved to Steenberg. At that time they were trying to get everybody out of the bush. They would come around at one o' clock in the morning. They would even bulldoze at night. Dishes would be broken, everything would be turned upside down. I would have liked to have stayed where I charred, but I couldn't and still be with my children. And the employers would have to register me, but I wouldn't do this because of the pass. I thought it best to live in the shack but spend as little time as possible in it. Each night I would come home and leave two children in the pondok — I sent one back to relatives in the Ciskei. Then I would take some blankets and just go to sleep under some bushes outside.'

'Even in the rain?'

'The rain, the wind, nothing. I didn't care. I did this for three years. When the inspectors would go into the shack one of my sons, who speaks good Afrikaans, would say that he was a "coloured" and that his mother and father had died long ago. There were times when I didn't think I was going to make it, when I almost gave up. But it is only now that I do not feel so strong anymore. If I was a few years younger, I would still go out and char. But now two of my sons are working on the sea, so they are helping me out. I would not be afraid of the future if I was younger. Now, though, I am tired. I do not think that I can take another move.'

Mrs. Zonwabela Mcaphukiso had been arrested the week before we spoke with her as she was walking to Belhar for water.

'We are happy to obey white people when they are serving our interests. But it appears that they only want us in this Cape Town if you stay with the "madams". Nobody is obliged to respect people who do not have respect for you. This applies to us and the white people. In fact, we are tired of all their nonsense.

'Before, things used not to be like this. Our fathers had wonderful times and were loyal to their wives. The white people have corrupted the simple life we had before. When I travel to the Transkei and to places where people lived with little interference from white people, I see the land is now divided and people can no longer live on the land. South Africa is for all of us and there should be no question of being forced to live at a certain confined place. No white person is forced against his will to go back to his place of origin.'

'Where are you from?'

'From this Cape Town. I was born here yet I still cannot be here. For when I divorced my second husband they stamped my pass and told me to marry to get a house. I became a sub-tenant in the townships. But as a lodger, all that goes wrong in the house is blamed on you. It is as if the others who live there can do nothing wrong. You have very little protection. People are against registering you as a sub-tenant for then after you help them with the rent, they can just tell you to go away. This happens very frequently.

'I stayed in many different houses. My children were just scattered all over the show and sometimes I would go a long time without seeing some of them. This has hurt me. Whenever I see them misbehaving, I think that if they had grown up closely in my hands, there would have been a difference. Sometimes I stayed in the Flats (men's single quarters). I was arrested there three times and had to pay R5 each time. However the greater risk was for the man. When I was caught with him he had to pay R30 and was in danger of losing his room.

'This became too much for us to bear. I was working as a nurse's assistant — a job which demands that one must not be too tired. You are supposed to be warm and hospitable. When I would go to work I would already feel tired and irritated and would fight with everybody. I had no place where I could rest. When I went to the doctors they told me that I was becoming sick because I was worrying too much. They said that I needed a place to rest and be left alone. Here, where I am now, I am able to relax and cool my nerves. And although I have had to give up my job at the hospital, I have been able to sell paraffin, sweets and vegetables, and I find life here more peaceful than in the townships.'

A SERVANT

Whites who visited the camp were often brought to see Mrs. Jane Sibisi. Her English was precise, she was carefully dressed, and she would always say apologetically that she wished she had a better place to entertain her guests.

Yet most of the squatters had little patience with her because they said she thought herself superior to them, having lived and worked for years in a white home in Cape Town.

At first Mrs. Sibisi did not reveal how overwhelmed she was by what had happened to her. But when she spoke of her past, she became anxious. One day she went to a box and took out the pictures of the house where she had once worked — a small 'Cape Dutch' home with whitewashed walls and a thatched roof. She also found pictures of her old employers. One shot was of the teaching staff of the Accra Secondary School, taken in 1947. Her employer, then stationed in Ghana in the British civil service, was wearing a white suit — the perfect English colonial.

Mrs. Sibisi symbolized pathetically the plight of the people of Modderdam: they had been brought to town to serve the white man, and when this was done, they were expected to leave. This Mrs. Sibisi had done so well — even to the extent of losing contact with other Africans as she tried hard to acquire not only the language but the habits and attitudes of white Cape Town. This made her eviction from the city terrifying.

'I am a woman who was insulated from the problems of Africans for many years. I worked and lived with a family that was very good to me. My master and his wife brought me into their house and were like a father and mother to me. I was a woman from the country who had come here in search of a husband who had deserted me. They gave me a job, and I was not treated like most servants. When they had coffee, I had coffee. They used to tell me always that I was one of the family and I began to feel that way too. The husband taught me English until I could speak it well. The wife taught me knitting and sewing. I had all my needs cared for. When I began in 1958 I was getting R8, which was very good for those days. By the time I had to leave I received R70, which is also quite high. Occasionally I would go on holiday to the country and sometimes I would visit people in the township, but most of the time I was in the house in Kensington. I felt very secure all those years.

'Then in 1970 the husband fell sick and died. Before his death, though, he asked me to stay and take care of his wife as she too was not well. This I did until she became too ill for me to care for properly. Then she was taken to a nursing home, and the house and all that was in it was sold.

'For the first time in fifteen years I found myself on my own. I did not want to look for another domestic job as I still wanted to visit the wife frequently. She had very little money to give me, however, for it had all gone to the nursing home. But as I had promised the husband, I decided that I would stay with her until she passed away. I decided that I wanted to live in Langa, but at the superintendent's office they told me that I must first marry. Now, this is not an easy thing just to find a husband when you are no longer young. It is better not to marry just for convenience.

'But I was able to find a man. Not one of these Xhosas who I

47

think are often rude to their women, but a good Zulu who had just lost his wife and was looking for another one. We returned to the superintendent's office and we were then pressed for every little detail. They demanded our marriage certificate, and then the death certificate from the other wife. But we knew that they must have those documents already. It became clear to us that they didn't want to give us a house even though both of us qualify for one. We had no choice but to come out here. This has taught me that as an African when you think you are safe, you are really not. My old employers would be very hurt if they saw me here, but the wife is now no longer clear in the head and I do not want to worry her by telling her.'

PART 2
The Road to Modderdam

4. The Early Cape

Many of the men and women of Modderdam came to the camp because poverty, sickness and loneliness pushed them from their villages to Cape Town, and white laws threatened to drive them from Cape Town back to the rural areas. Apartheid to them was thus a profound and terrifying contradiction in which their old culture in the village and the new one in the city were being destroyed.

This plight was, in essence, the plight of Africans throughout the long years of white rule. The roots of the system which brought the squatters to Modderdam reach back to the seventeenth, eighteenth and nineteenth centuries. It was to this history that the current government turned to sanction the demolition of the camp.

KHOI-SAN

The Cape Peninsula was once an island separated from the rest of Africa. When the oceans receded, perhaps 5 000 years ago, they left a forty-mile ridge of low mountains connected by sand flats and dunes to a taller chain forty miles away. Forests and thick pastures lined the mountain slopes, and bitter-almond trees and thorn bushes covered the valley. The wild life of Africa prospered on the Peninsula and throughout the Western Cape. It was cool and rainy in winter, warm and dry in summer. Throughout the year, and particularly in February and March, strong winds from the southeast whipped across the shores.

The Bushmen or San, short people with curly hair and yellow-brown skin, lived in the mountains, hunting game with poisoned arrows and gathering roots, nuts, locusts, and other plants and grubs. Tribes of Khoi-khoi or Hottentots lived in the valleys, where they herded cattle and produced iron.

The Khoi-khoi were the masters in this sparsely populated corner of Africa. The San came down from their caves to work for them — hunting their game and helping them in battle. The wealthiest Khoi-khoi tribes had two or three hundred men and women, and flocks of over ten thousand sheep and cattle.

The Khoi-san people may have been descendants of the prehistoric races of men who evolved in southern Africa. The skin colour and physiognomy of the Khoi-san also suggest that they may have been related to the Amharics of Ethiopia, having migrated down the East Coast, across the Congo basin, and along the coasts of what is now Angola and Namibia.

WHITES

When Jan van Riebeeck of the Dutch East India Company landed at the foot of Table Mountain to establish a rest station for ships bound for the east, he found small bands of Khoi-khoi on the beach. They had few cattle but they told van Riebeeck that two wealthy tribes, the Goringkona and the Saldanhers, passed by Table Bay each year in early summer and late fall as they walked their flocks from Saldanha Bay on the Atlantic to Cape Agulhas on the Indian Ocean.

The Dutch were initially satisfied with the price, number, and quality of the livestock they received later that year. Yet after three years of bartering, the Khoi had had their fill of Dutch goods and would cull only a few heads from the flock to sell.

The trade was further threatened when the Khoi and the San began to steal cattle and destroy the crops of the settlement as the Dutch established their own herds and grazed them throughout the year on land the Khoi once used freely.

The first attempt by the Dutch to protect themselves from the country's inhabitants was a doomed scheme to turn the Cape Peninsula back into an island. In early 1656, van Riebeeck surveyed the Cape Flats to see if it was possible to build a canal from the Indian to the Atlantic Ocean. He soon concluded, however, that the project was foolish — for while it might protect the colony from an invasion, it would also cut off its food supply. The early wish to cut off the colony from the rest of Africa now seems more significant than it may have been when it was first expressed, for it symbolizes well the contradiction between white fear and white needs.

The canal was never built. Yet after skirmishes over land and cattle developed into a small war in 1660, the Dutch erected three watchtowers at the edge of the Cape Flats and later linked them with transplanted bitter-almond trees, fast-growing brambles and thorn bushes. Van Riebeeck predicted enthusiastically that the 'protective fence' would make it impossible for cattle or sheep to be smuggled in or out of the colony and that the movements of the Khoi-khoi and San could now be monitored closely. Thus six years after the settlers arrived, a rudimentary pass system was established in order to control, but not eliminate the contact with the 'Hottentots'.

Yet attempts to keep the Khoi-san outside the fence were abandoned after Van Riebeeck returned to Holland. The new company commander, Simon van der Stel, moved across the Flats in 1679 to establish Stellenbosch at the foot of the Hottentot-Hollands. The colony was divided into four sections, and one was called Moddergate (watershed) or Modderdam. It was so named because rain and mountain streams flooded the land in winter.

SLAVES

Slaves were soon brought to the colony to meet growing labour demands. One hundred and seventy girls and boys from Angola landed at De Kaap on March 28, 1658 aboard the Dutch ship Amersfoort. Van Riebeeck was disappointed to find them too young and ill to be of much use to the colony, yet 228 more West African slaves were brought to shore a few months later. These stronger, older men were quickly put to work, but they soon absconded — some even in the chains which bound their feet. The Dutch feared that the Khoi and the slaves were in cahoots. Van Riebeeck warned the Khoi chiefs that the West Africans would soon be armed and would rob and murder them. 'The slaves would also multiply,' he told them, 'and might become masters of all the Hottentots.'[1] This was the earliest attempt by whites to divide and rule.

Many of the Khoi-khoi and San fled into the interior, but those who did not were also pressed into service. They quickly lost their cattle, and the culture which had been built around the use and worship of their herds deteriorated. They began to intermarry with whites and slaves and became the first 'coloureds', although they were then referred to as Basters. More slaves were also imported, not from West Africa but from East Africa and the East Indies.

By the middle of the eighteenth century, farms and villages had been built throughout the Western Cape, where ten thousand slaves lived among eight thousand whites. A slave hierarchy developed which resembled that which now exists among blacks. Africans, the lowest class, worked in the fields. Basters were home servants. The Muslims from the East were the skilled craftsmen who built the expansive plantation homes with the sloped gables which became the stamp of Cape Dutch architecture. Many of these 'Malays', as they were called, bought their freedom.

The presence of slaves enabled the colonists to become a landed gentry, yet the colony was nonetheless in constant debt. In 1772, when the Dutch East India Company was near collapse, the directors questioned whether it had been wise to build a slave culture in the Cape. 'I believe it would have been better,' Baron Gutsch van Imhoff wrote, 'had we, when this colony was established, commenced with Europeans and brought them hither in such numbers that hunger and want would have forced them to work. But having imported slaves, every common ordinary European becomes a gentleman and prefers to be served than to work . . . In addition, the majority of the farmers in the colony are not farmers in the real sense of the word, but owners of the plantations, and many of them consider it a shame to work with their own hands.'[2]

A PASS LAW

As long as it was possible to import slaves, the free Khoi-khoi who still lived in the Western Cape were allowed to travel and settle at will. Yet when the slave trade was terminated in 1806, eight years after the British first occupied the Colony, the whites prevented them from bargaining for their labour. In 1809, all 'Hottentots' and 'Basters' were prohibited from travelling from one magisterial district to another without a permit. Three years later a further law was passed requiring children who had lived on a plantation for their first eight years to work for another ten — thus keeping the parents in service as well.

These ordinances were South Africa's earliest pass laws. They helped resolve the immediate labour shortage, but also provoked the country's first anti-pass campaign. Members of the London and Wesleyan missionary societies attacked the legislation and offered the Khoi-khoi refuge in mission stations and villages throughout the colony. The missionaries' protests were remarkable in their similarity to those used 170 years later by opponents of the pass system. They argued that the pass laws, by keeping the price of labour artificially low, not only led to 'Hottentot' poverty but to economic stagnation throughout the colony. 'The abettors of the present system seem never to have contemplated the aboriginal of the country as a consumer,' wrote John Phillip, the most virulent and effective critic of the laws.[3]

The missionaries tied the abolition of the ordinances to the anti-slavery movement throughout the Empire. They won their case in 1828, when all but slaves had the right to move freely. Many workers left for Cape Town or assumed a nomadic life as vagrants and casual workers in the countryside. The labour crisis was made even more acute in 1834 when all slaves were freed. Farmers attempted to reinstate the pass laws and apply them to the freed slaves as well. However these new bills were vetoed by colonial authorities in London.

XHOSA

The arrival of Xhosa-speaking workers in the Western Cape was in part a response to the freeing of the Hottentots and the slaves. These men, ancestors of the Africans now living in Cape Town, were themselves descended from tribes in Central and West Africa which first migrated to southern Africa around the year 500. They lived along the Indian Ocean coast in villages which extended to the Gamtoos River, 250 miles from the Cape Peninsula. They had not settled in the south west corner of the continent, historians believe, because the sorghum, maize, pumpkin and calabashes they cultivated would not grow in the semi-desert and sour grasslands which lay between the river and the pastures of the Western Cape.[4]

These tribes lived among the Khoi-khoi and the San. Their culture, too, centred around livestock.

Their central ritual and economic transaction was *lobola,* the 'buying' of wives with cattle. Class distinctions were established and maintained by this exchange as richer men traded among themselves to amass both wives and cattle while the poorer were prevented from establishing a large family for want of cattle, and from obtaining cattle for want of a large family.

The stability of this rural class system was maintained by the availability of land. When a clan became too large, the chief sanctioned marriages from within the lineage, and a new kraal was established. A chief's power was also checked by the ability of his people to pick up and leave. The poorer men and women could set off by themselves to establish their own homesteads. Both the oral history of the Xhosa and the reports of travellers and explorers confirm that for centuries the society had undergone little change. Rituals first described in the fifteenth century by Portuguese explorers were still intact to the finest detail three hundred years later. It was the remnants of this culture which the squatters brought to Modderdam.

Forty-five colonists set out from Stellenbosch in 1702 and met the Xhosa along the Gamtoos. During the following years, settlers came to build farms. The region, however, was more densely populated than the Cape Peninsula and the pioneers fought continually for the land. The whites feared the collusion of the Xhosa, Khoi-khoi and San as Van Riebeeck had been alarmed by the cooperation of the Khoi-khoi and the slaves. The different tribes *did* unite at times to raid white farms and villages — events which foreshadowed the cooperation of their coloured and African descendants two hundred years later. Yet the Xhosa, who bore the brunt of the fighting, were slowly pushed back. By 1770, they had retreated 300 miles to the Fish River. Eight years later, in an attempt to stop the border wars, the commander of the Cape Colony, Wilhelm van Plettenberg, drew a boundary along the Fish. It was, however, no more successful than earlier borders, and the whites moved steadily eastward during the next eight years, crossing the Keiskamma, the Ovimzubu, and finally the Kei.

Van Plettenberg's line assumed more significance in the twentieth century. For when the Afrikaner descendants of the Cape farmers tried to re-erect barriers between themselves and the Africans in the 1940s and 1950s, they used the Fish River as a guide.

The gradual conquest of the Xhosa began their conversion into a labour force. Different clans competed for increasingly scarce pastures. Classes in the villages became more rigid as large clans could no longer divide and build new kraals. Poor villagers could not find land to establish their own wealth and became increasingly dependent on the chief. In the early years of the nineteenth century, some chiefs urged these men to work on white farms alongside the Khoi-khoi and the slaves. Xhosa society was shaken more profoundly than at any other time in its history. The humiliation and growing poverty of a people who had lived in harmony with their environment for so long led men and women to hunt for witches. Unable to explain the debacle, they began to believe that the true enemy lay within their own people. Throughout the early decades of the nineteenth century, prophets and sangomas toured the land calling for great purification sacrifices of cattle and crops and announcing the coming of an apocalypse.

The last great war was fought from 1848 to 1852. The Xhosa lost more men and land than in any previous campaign as they were pushed back to the Kei, 500 miles from where they had initially met the whites on the Gamtoos. This final defeat provoked a witch-hunt and a messianic vision far grander than any which had preceded it. In March, 1856, a sixteen-year-old girl, Nonquase, saw her ancestors on the shores of the Kei where she had gone to fetch water. When she returned, she told her father, Makhaza, who followed her back to the river. He too saw the shades. They ordered him to sacrifice cattle, to purify himself and to return to the spot three days later.

Makhaza saw his dead brother when he visited the river for the second time. He told Makhaza that the dead Xhosa warriors would be restored and the whites driven from the land if his people destroyed their cattle and burned their crops. Then two blood red suns would appear in the sky and a hurricane would cleanse the land, sweeping the whites into the sea. After the storm, new crops would appear, the cattle would live again and the fallen Xhosa would be resurrected. The land would be theirs again.

Nonquase travelled throughout the country delivering the prophecy, whipping the people into a frenzy of expectation. After almost a year of preaching, February 18, 1857 was set as the date for the great sacrifice. Several thousand cattle were slaughtered that day and fields upon fields of maize and sorghum were set ablaze. When the blood suns and the hurricane did not come, Nonquase and other prophets blamed the failure on villagers who had refused to destroy everything. As each day passed, the pressure to burn more and more crops and kill more and more cattle grew. The sacrifice continued for three months, and the people starved. West of the Kei alone, it was estimated that between 68 000 and 100 000 people died. The spell finally snapped in May and the survivors staggered onto white farms in the Eastern and Western Cape, begging for food, shelter, and work. Nonquase became a squatter on a white farm, where she lived out her life. The British soon annexed the rest of the Transkei without a struggle, and the trek of the Xhosa to white lands began in earnest.

5. Africans in Town

Ninety-eight years after Xhosa men and women came looking for refuge in white farms and towns, the South African government announced a plan to return all Africans in the Western Cape to the once prosperous lands of the Transkei and Ciskei. Twenty years after this removal scheme had begun, the squatter camp along Modderdam Road was demolished and many of the residents were ordered back to the rural areas.

This plan to 'purify' the region was provoked by the diamond and gold discoveries during the last third of the nineteenth century. The link between African miners in Johannesburg and other mining centres and African squatters in Cape Town is explicit. For it was the creation of a huge African working class in the north which ultimately led the government to envision a haven free from Africans in the south.

MIGRANT LABOUR

The first diamond mines were open pits where any white, African, or coloured could bring a shovel and pocket his find. An African missionary, Gwayi Tyamzashe, reported after his first visit there in 1872 that 'when they are all at work, you can hardly distinguish the whites from the coloured, for they all resemble the diamondiferous soil they are working.'[1] Tyamzashe described his visit in a missionary-run newspaper, the *Kaffir Express*. (The paper, which later changed its name to the *Christian Express* and then to *South African Outlook*, has carefully reported the impact

57

of mining and industry on black life.)

Yet once the top layer of diamonds was skimmed, large work crews and elaborate machinery were needed to filter the soil and wash the diamonds. Only eight years after the first gem was found, 10 000 blacks were working in the new town of Kimberley. Tyamzashe reported in 1874: 'There are Bushmen, Korannas, Hottentots, Griqua, Batlaping, Damaras, Barolong, Barotse, Bahatla, Bakwena, Bamangwatu, Bapedi, Magalaka, Batsuetla, Baganana, Basuto, Magwaba, Mazulu, Maswazi, Matsetswa, Matonga, Matebele, Mabaca, Mampondo, Mamfengu, Batembu, Maxosa.'[2]

Despite the white conquest of African lands and kingdoms, most mineworkers still had some property and could only be drawn from their kraals for a few months at a time. Each man received a three or six month contract, during which time he was housed in a closed compound. With the discovery of the Transvaal gold reefs in the 1880s, the migrant labour system grew vastly. Recruiters combed villages throughout South Africa and as far away as Tanzania and Angola.

The thirst for labour was astonishing. By the turn of the century, about fifty percent of all men in the Transkei and Ciskei had done time in the mines. When wages were not sufficient to draw more villagers from their kraals, labour taxes were levied to force them into service. ' . . . We are now to be driven to work even if we do not consider the pay good enough,' men told missionary J. Brownlee Ross when a new tax was proposed in 1895.[3] Another missionary, Godfrey Calloway, visited the Transkei fifteen years later and found that as he stepped out of the train all he saw was the word 'i-joyini' — a slang Xhosa term for labour recruiting. It dwarfed every other advertisement, he said, staring at him in red, black or blue letters from corrugated iron roofs, store windows and office walls. 'You not only see it everywhere but you also hear it. You meet it in the smoking room in the store, in the Magistrate's office and wherever men gather.'[4]

A migrant was in many ways the ideal worker in an industry which needed massive cheap labour. He made few demands on the employer or the town in which he lived. He could withstand the brutal conditions in the compound because he only wanted to do his time and go home. This was comfort to the employer who saw the migrant as a man with aspirations as foreign as the language he spoke and the witchdoctor who treated him. The black man thus found his patience, and the white man his authority, in the knowledge that the migrant would return to his village.

White preference for this unthreatening worker was stated graphically by a labour recruiter in 1907 who advised his company that 'The raw, untutored unclad Kafirs, fresh from their kraals in the mountains are the best and most trustworthy workers. The contact of civilization is invariably pernicious and demoralizing to the peculiar organization of our Kafir friends . . . Above all, mistrust a Kafir who speaks English and wears trousers.'[5]

This image of the hard worker, in awe of the white man and his city, quickly became the stereotype of the 'good African'. Yet black rejection of the values of the migrant began almost as soon as they were established. The man who oscillated between his farm and the mines saw this life as temporary. If he could save enough money to invest in his kraal, he would be able to remain home for longer and longer periods. If the money was not sufficient, the length of his stay would grow and his link to his village would gradually fade.

By the beginning of the twentieth century, the dynamic of the migrant system was already shifting towards the towns. 'At present there is land for every male (in the Transkei),' the *Express* wrote in 1906, 'but in a few years the younger sons will have either to live as "poor blacks" dependent on the bounty of their more fortunate relatives, or what is more likely to happen, they will drift into the town locations.'[6] Thus as the whites were anxious to maintain the economic, legal, and psychological conditions which created the 'good African', blacks gradually looked to the city not only for work, but for land, family life and education.

NEW PASS LAWS

Perhaps if Africans had come alone to work in the new cities whites would not have resisted their settlement. Yet black migration was simultaneous with that of poor rural Afrikaners, many of whom had been forced to the cities by the devastation of the Boer War. Afrikaners were unwilling to do the menial jobs they called 'kafferwerk' because their equality with the black man in the labour market upset the long tradition of white domination. In 1907, Jan Hofmeyr explained to the Transvaal Indigency

Commission that the new white immigrants would often remain unemployed rather than work alongside Africans. 'Before the emancipation of slaves,' he said, 'all menial work was performed by the slaves, and the white men were in the position of a more-or-less non-labouring aristocracy. This tradition as to the place of the white man has persisted ever since.'[7]

This fear and bitterness towards African competition led white workers, as well as their employers, to insist that the barriers which had always distinguished the African from the 'European' be preserved — the black man who mastered the city and acquired urban aspirations became the stereotype of the 'bad African'. The preference of the 'good' migrant to the 'bad' settler thus prevented whites from facing the realization that as the cities grew, the old race distinctions would inevitably fade.

Forty years after the first diamonds were found, it had become difficult for labour recruiters to induce village men to come to town without their families. An official of the Native Recruiting Corporation told a commission in 1914 that he had met many men up country who had told him, 'Having lost my cattle, there is no tie to keep me here. My home is my work and I should like to have my wife and children with me at work.'[8]

WHITE CITIES

The urban African population in 1920 had tripled since the beginning of the century to over 600 000. The number of women immigrants was increasing rapidly. There were 25 men to every woman in town in 1895. Twenty-five years later, the number had dropped to six to one. The cultural, physical, and emotional barriers between blacks and whites *were* collapsing, leading whites to warn that South Africa was becoming 'mongrelized'. The Stallard Commission of the Transvaal Local Government warned in 1922 that in many city slums, forty or more small shacks were built in back yards which were 'packed to overflowing with every class and colour of Natives, coloured people, white people, Chinese and Indians, all mixed up and living together anyhow.'[9] Three years later, Jan Smuts, then leader of the Union Party, warned similarly that 'the Natives have gone into the towns, they have mixed with the rest of the population, they have not been segregated in their own areas, and . . . the most lamentable results have ensued in consequence.'[10] White civilization, Smuts said, had been dragged down and degraded.

While white rule was still unquestioned, and would be for another thirty years, an increasing number of whites began to associate black urbanization with the decline of white supremacy. They realized in fright that the wealthier the country became, the sooner the old order would fall.

It was in response to this agonizing dilemma that the principle which later became the basis for the ideology of apartheid was first established. The Stallard Commission at the end of its report recommended that:

> The Native should only be allowed to enter the urban areas, which are essentially the white man's creation, when he is willing to enter and to minister to the needs of the white man and should depart therefrom when he ceases so to minister.[11]

Yet this vision of a land of white cities and black villages was already obsolete. The belief that there was some method by which the country could grow while at the same time return to the days when migrant labour was unchallenged was an illusion which has still not been put to rest.

The first law regulating African life in the city was passed in 1923. It called for the segregation of those who had already arrived in town and laws to regulate new immigrants. These pass laws updated those first developed in the nineteenth century. While they were not strictly enforced, they provided the framework for all future legislation. Every man who arrived in town or who had lost his job was required to report to a 'Native superintendent' empowered to deport those found 'habitually unemployed, those who had no livelihood, and those who were idle, dissolute and disorderly.'[12]

The most significant section of the bill, however, was that which stripped Africans of the right to buy land in town. This regulation, more than any other, enabled whites to persist in seeing the cities as 'white areas' even as these cities acquired a black majority.

The Act was no more successful than any other white attempt to control black movement. During the great depression more Africans were driven off the land than ever before and the new African townships were quickly overwhelmed. Immigrant families lived as before in squatter camps and in white areas scattered throughout the cities. Once again, however, this new influx led to new enthusiasm for the migrant worker. The Depression also forced Afrikaners into the city in far greater numbers than had arrived at the turn of the century. One answer to high white unemployment, legislators believed, was the black migrant who could theoretically be brought in and out of town depending on white labour demand and the turn of the business cycle. Whereas the migrant system was initially a way to draw Africans off the land in times of growth, it could also be a means to keep them out of the cities when their labour was not needed. In 1929, Smuts called for registration and regulation of all women immigrants.[13] 'While the Native may be out of his own area for a limited period each year to work with a white employer, he will leave his wife and children behind in the Native home.'

This declaration again proved useless. The black urban population doubled in the fifteen years after the passage of the first Urban Areas Act. In some towns, there were only twice as many men as women. African immigration was irreversible, yet ironically, the very presence of the new families provoked a more desperate attempt to restore the migrant labour system and preserve the 'good African'. In 1936, new amendments to the Urban Areas Act were instituted that were far more complex and rigid than the original bill. An African could be expelled from a city in fourteen days if he could not find work. Employers were barred from hiring an African from outside the local labour area without government approval. Native superintendents were required to keep close records of labour supply and demand, and were authorized to close off an area to migration if there was a glut of workers in one town and a dearth in another. Both women and men were now required to obtain permission before leaving a village or entering a city. Those who had lived in town for over five years were permitted to stay for another five, but thereafter were to receive only yearly permits. Women who had entered illegally, as well as unemployed men, could be removed without a court order by police to their homes or to a prison farm.

Yet Africans again ignored these regulations. South Africa entered World War II in 1939, setting off a labour demand unequalled since the heady first days of the gold rush. The increasingly hopelesss contradiction between the economic forces pulling Africans permanently to the cities and the political forces driving them out is best reflected in the pass arrest records during the first years of the war. Three hundred thousand men were fined, arrested, or deported at a time when employers clamoured for workers.

WHITE PROTEST

Despite the desperate attempts to preserve the migrant system, there were those whites who foresaw the transformation of the 'raw untutored Native' into a 'detribalized' worker and called for the removal of the pass laws and other residency restrictions. They challenged the stereotype of the 'good African' and argued that if the immigration of African families was accepted, a stable working class could be established. The *Express* argued in 1907 that the problem with the 'urban Native' was not that he was too settled, but that he was not settled enough.[14] 'At his home,' the paper observed, 'the Native is subject to many familiar laws and customs. The social unit is the *umzi* or village. The laws which regulate village life are well-defined. They relate to such things as family life, obedience to the chief's authority, cleanliness, respect to elders and hospitality, and they tend to maintain a well-ordered social life.'

By contrast, the paper continued, there are few restraints in the town. 'The Native has no security of tenure, no garden, no incentive to improve his home. In many cases he has no home at all, but only a lodging place which is often a miserable hovel or shanty.' As a result, the African had a freedom thrust upon him for which he was 'wholly unprepared.' The paper concluded that only by allowing wives and children into the towns could the values of the village be maintained. 'The remedy is to provide the conditions which will make this family life possible and to lay on the town Native the responsibility for his own social order which he would have in village life.'[15]

Fifteen years later, the *Express* warned that the migrant labour system was gradually destroying the African family. The paper's protests closely foreshadowed those of whites and Africans made fifty years later. 'Anyone coming into contact with the Native people at their homes is forced to realize the harm that is being done to Native family life by the repeated and prolonged absences from home of the men who work at the mines, the docks, the railways and the city stores.' Boys leave at seventeen, the paper charged, and are away until they are middle-aged, with only short intervals at home to rest and plough their little plots. In order to save money, some even starve themselves in the hostels. And while many remain 'sober men and faithful to their wives', it is not surprising that others fail. ' "Where is your husband?" you ask some poor woman. "He is at the mines." "When did he go?" "Three years ago." "Does he send you money?" "No'm." "What is the matter? Is he drinking?" "I hear so." '[16]

By the 1920s, civil servants, legislators, a few trade unionists and some businessmen had joined missionaries in calling for an end to the migrant system. They realized that the urban African would never be able to return to his village. James Henderson submitted evidence to a government commission in 1926 showing the extent to which regions of the Ciskei had deteriorated during the fifty years in which the men of the villages had been working in the mines. In one relatively fertile district, population had grown from 5 600 to 12 000 between 1875 and 1926. Yet at the same time, sales of wool, hides and other animal products had dropped by £7 000; sales of grain had halved as had purchases of farm equipment. At the same time, purchases of basic foodstuffs had tripled. 'It is without question the income from the labour centres that keeps the congested areas going,' Henderson testified.[17]

In words which anticipate the protests of the Cape Town squatters in the 1970s, Henderson described how the use of migrant labour had shifted from a system which helped build African wealth to one that insured African poverty.[18] 'Were the wages needed, as probably in earlier times was the case, only to supplement nearly adequate home-produced supplies, they would be of incalculable advantage for developing the people, but when they are required to support families in remote Native communities who have to buy at credit prices even the staple articles of diet, they do not suffice. They enable the families to drag along, but they do not solve the problems of livelihood for the future. The Native outlook is thus bleak, in many cases near to hopelessness.'

Each successive attempt to ignore, deny or arrest African immigration provoked new protests by a continually growing number of whites. The term 'liberal' came to stand for those who called for the acceptance of the permanency of the African working class. The Institute of Race Relations was established in 1939 to promote the rights of blacks in the city. Its founder, A J Hoernlé, stated firmly that 'the urban African has his home in the town as truly as the European. Most urban African families could not return to the land and make a living there, even if they want to. They and their families live, in so far as their low income permits, a life which is, in principle, indistinguishable from the European way of living.'[19]

The government finally began to listen to its critics during World War II. A committee under Robert Smit urged that the pass laws be scrapped, the migrant system dismantled, urban land rights granted, and restrictions on union organizing lifted — in short, that the African work force be treated like workers in other industrializing nations. The bill was never passed, but prominent members of the ruling United Party supported it. Jan Smuts, once a strong proponent of 'Stallardism', recanted. 'Nothing can now prevent further African settlement,' he conceded in 1946. 'We tried segregation but that has not stopped it in the least. The process has been accelerated. You might as well try to keep the ocean back with a broom.'[20]

1948

The white debate over the African working class came to a head after the war. Despite the massive migration between 1939 and 1945, virtually no African housing was built. The black population of Johannesburg alone increased by 100 000 yet only 1 000 new homes were constructed. This shortage led to the greatest squatter movements the country had ever seen. An entire squatter political party was organized to seize land, set up new shanty towns, and force the government to provide services. It was named 'Sofasonke' ('we suffer together'). James 'Sofasonke' Mpanza was its leader. On a Sunday in March, 1944, he led more than ten thousand people to open ground outside Newclare, a suburb of Johannesburg. By Monday morning, when the white inspectors came to work, they found rows of shacks made of canvas and wood. Mpanza called the camp Shanty Town. Alan Paton wrote of it in *Cry the Beloved Country*, calling Mpanza 'Mr Dubula':

This night they are busy in Orlando. At one house after another the lights are burning. I shall carry the iron, and you my wife the child, and you my two sons, two poles and you my small one, bring as many sacks as you are able, down to the land by the railway lines. Many people are moving there, you can hear the sound of digging and hammering already. It is good that the night is warm, that there is no rain. Thank you, Mr Dubula, we are satisfied with this piece of ground. Thank you, Mr Dubula, here is our shilling for the committee.[21]

Once Shanty Town was established, Mpanza became the leader and adviser of several more squatter movements. Six settlements were built for over 200 families. There were innumerable smaller camps. When police attempted to break down the shacks, the squatters simply moved a quarter of a mile away and re-erected them. Mpanza took on some of the trappings of an African chief come to town. He toured the settlements on a white horse and surrounded himself with bodyguards. Every Sunday, he gave long speeches. The shanty towns were later replaced by brick houses which together formed the South Western Townships (Soweto). Mpanza became known as the 'father of Soweto'.

The boldness and omnipresence of squatters throughout the cities of South Africa was a central issue in the parliamentary election of 1948. During a contest unusual in the clarity of its choices, the white electorate was asked to determine the future of urban Africans. Either the government would persist in its attempt to maintain the pass laws and the vestiges of the migrant system or it would finally discard the controls on African settlement which had developed throughout the twentieth century. The former course would lead to greater and greater legal and political pressure against city blacks; the latter would result in greater integration, higher wages, and ultimately, the granting of African political rights in town.

The United Party, finally freeing itself of the lure of 'Stallardism', endorsed in its platform the findings of a government commission led by Justice D H Fagan which concluded that 'the idea of total segregation is utterly impracticable' and that 'the townward movement of Natives is simply an economic phenomenon which is also occurring with regard to other races . . .'[22] This drift, Fagan advised, 'can be guided and regulated but it is impossible to prevent it or to turn it in the opposite direction.' As if to make sure that the implications of this immigration were fully understood, the Commission stressed that there were not only migrant workers in the urban areas, but also a settled, permanent Native population.'

The opposition National Party, campaigning hard for the votes of Afrikaner workers, responded by elevating the Stallard Doctrine into the full-blown ideology of 'apartheid' — 'separateness'. The campaign manifesto called yet again for a return to the labour patterns of the early mining days:

> The Bantu in the urban areas should be regarded as migratory citizens not entitled to political or social rights equal to those of the Whites. The process of detribalisation should be arrested. The entire migration of Bantu into and from the cities would be controlled by municipal bodies. Migration into and from the reserves should likewise be strictly controlled. Redundant Bantu in the urban centres should be returned to their original habitat in the country areas or the reserves. Bantu from the country areas or the reserves should be admitted to the European cities or towns only as temporary employees, obliged to return to their homes after the expiry of their employment. 'For this pupose, a convenient identification and control system will have to be devised.[23]

The National Party won the election by a narrow margin. Six years later, it announced that Cape Town would be the first city to be free of Africans.

6. Apartheid

As the new government's policies were articulated in the late forties and fifties, it became clear that the ideology of apartheid was an elaborate attempt to answer the fears of African domination created by the growth of cities by returning to the physical and social division which had existed one, two and three hundred years earlier. One might have thought that Cape Town would have been exempted from the new programme because its history had differed so sharply from the rest of the country. Whereas Africans had become the majority in most cities, in the Western Cape they comprised only ten percent of the population.

Yet ironically, Cape Town and the surrounding region were chosen as the model zone for apartheid. Precisely *because* the number of Africans was relatively small the planners argued that the policy could be implemented there with rapid progress: the experiment could then serve as an example to the rest of the country. Building apartheid from Cape Town was also symbolically important. As the oldest area of white settlement, it was the only place where whites had arrived before black-skinned Africans. 'Cleansing' the Western Cape would be a way for whites to reclaim what was rightfully theirs.

Yet the Nationalists, like their predecessors, were gradually forced to abandon this vision because they could not do without African labour. Twenty-five years after the Party had come to power, the ideology had shifted from the call to send African workers from the city to a justification for keeping them there with as few rights as possible. This, in turn, only succeeded in impoverishing the old African lands to an even greater degree.

CLEANSING THE CAPE

The Xhosa men who had come to the farms and roadgangs of the Western Cape in the 1840s, 50s and 60s left in large numbers to join other Africans in the rush for diamonds and gold. Yet by the turn of the century, workers who were too old, tired, bitter, or afraid to work in the mines came again to the region. The docks and railroads were expanding rapidly. From 1891 to 1904, the African population grew from under one thousand to over seven thousand. Single men who found work on the docks lived in hostels along Table Bay, not far from where the old slave lodge had stood. Other men and women were scattered throughout the city.

Cape Town whites first became alarmed by the presence of Africans after an outbreak of bubonic plague in 1902. The city council constructed a 'location' on the Cape Flats, three miles from the centre of the city. Shacks of corrugated iron were pushed together in an inverted V. A well was dug, and 'night-soil' sanitation was supplied. The rent was nominal. The location was called 'N'dabeni' ('free ground').

N'dabeni was a 'temporary' location, but the municipality built nothing more permanent and soon it, too, became a health hazard. During the 1918 flu epidemic, many whites called for the camp's demolition and the construction of a new location further out on the Flats which would have paved roads, brick houses, hostels for migrants, sports grounds, and schools. Langa, named for the Zulu warrior Langalibalele, was founded in 1923 under the provisions of the new Urban Areas Act. By 1930, ten thousand people lived in the township which quickly became a centre for the new urban African society. Life was built around church, school, sports clubs and political organizations. The leaders were not chiefs but the mission-educated teachers, doctors and other white-collar workers. The other residents came to call these people the 'ooscuse me' for the way in which they aped white manners and aspirations. The 'ooscuse-me' in turn dismissed the migrants as hicks. The residents of Langa saw themselves as superior to the newer African immigrants who continued to build squatter camps throughout the Cape Flats.[1]

The African population of the city doubled in the Thirties and again during the war. With housing shortages as severe as in Johannesburg, Africans went off into the bush like the followers of Mpanza. They lived among coloureds who were also coming off farms into the city. By the time the National Party came to power, 25 000 of the 36 000 Africans in the city were living in one of thirty squatter camps. The coloureds and Africans had begun to form a common culture, just as the Khoi-khoi had once merged with the East and West African slaves and with the Xhosa.

EISELEN LINE

The grand apartheid scheme for Cape Town was nothing less than the complete removal of all Africans in the Western Cape. This massive project, unveiled by Secretary of Native Affairs W.W.M. Eiselen in 1954, was an attempt to restore the racial makeup of the early Cape and thus prevent the collusion of coloureds and Africans and ensure the passivity of the migrant worker.

Eiselen was convinced that it was possible to save the good villager from 'corruption' in the city. Both in the squatter camps and on the job, he warned, the African quickly became part of a common black working class. 'The Native who works in a hotel or boarding house associates on an equal, and very soon, an intimate footing with the female coloured servants,' he warned. 'Their respective quarters are often situated close together and it is usually only a matter of time before cohabitation takes place. Under such conditions, the Native, who today is received and welcomed as an honest and trustworthy worker, must in time learn the less estimable "city tricks". In consequence he will no longer be a desirable type of worker.'[2]

Eiselen was also convinced, as the government was in the 1930s and 40s, that it was possible to turn the flow of African labour on and off at will. 'Where additional Native manpower is absolutely necessary,' Eiselen said, 'it should be obtained in the form of migrant labour which can easily return home when its services are no longer required in the Western Province.'[3]

The Eiselen Plan, as the removal scheme became known, was a simple denial that the process of industrialization and integration which had taken place since the turn of the century would continue. Eiselen and the other principal architect of the project, the future Prime Minister Hendrik Verwoerd, rejected the claim that this process was inevitable. Thirty years after whites first saw in industrialization an ultimate threat to their power, these two men and other ideologists saw with far greater clarity that white supremacy could only be preserved if somehow blacks could be prevented from acquiring the aspirations of a settled working class. Such a scheme might seem desperate and cruel, but the alternative was capitulation.

As a test of their ultimate ability to preserve white civilization, the Nationalists drew the Eiselen line near the Fish River — the place where van Plettenberg had first tried to separate the whites and the Africans. No new African settlement could occur inside the line. Those men, women and children who were born in the Western Cape and had lived there for fifteen years, or had worked for one employer for ten years, would be allowed to stay temporarily. All others would have to leave, with the exception of employed men who could stay on without their families in single quarters.

As there were over one hundred thousand African workers, the migrant labour system was the key to the scheme — and by extension, to the whole system of apartheid. Both Verwoerd and Eiselen claimed that it would be possible to make Cape Town a city whose African work force was exclusively migrant. Then mechanization and a growing coloured population would make these workers redundant, and they could be sent back to the Transkei and Ciskei. To facilitate this process, coloureds would be given preferential hiring throughout the region. The migrant system would be extended from the mining industry to every other sector of the economy. If not, Verwoerd argued, there would come a time when African labour would no longer be needed, but could not be uprooted. 'When a factory is reorganized,' he told Parliament, 'certain labour can be reduced or removed. If automation is introduced into a factory, manual labour can in many instances be eliminated.' However, he said, should Africans join unions or establish themselves firmly in any other way in the city, it would become impossible to dislodge them. 'This is the difference between labour we can remove and labour which has become so interwoven in so many ways in the white community, that it cannot be removed even if we want to.'[4] Verwoerd did not deny that such a programme would disrupt African families but he insisted that this could not be avoided because the future of white society in South Africa was at stake. If the government was strong enough in its resolve, Verwoerd predicted, it would be possible to reverse the flow from village to city by 1978.

The central piece of legislation used to implement the removal programme was a 1951 version of the 1936 pass law. For the first time, women as well as men were required to carry passes. Under section ten of the bill, an African was permitted in a city for more than three days only if he or she was (a) born in that city (b) had lived there for fifteen years or worked for one employer continuously for ten years (c) was under sixteen or (d) received special government dispensation. A person's status could not change through marriage. Thus a rural woman who married a '10 (1a)' man could be forced to leave the city upon her husband's death.

The police began arresting women in the streets and buses of Cape Town in early 1954. 'Influx control is operated even more strictly in the Western Cape than it is elsewhere in the Union,'[5] the Institute of Race Relations reported in its annual survey.

The removal scheme was also reflected in housing policy. Verwoerd vetoed the Cape Town City Council's plans to build new family housing in Langa for squatters and ordered hostels to be constructed in their place. In defending this action, Verwoerd once again recalled the stereotype of the 'good African'. 'It is peculiar but true,' he told a group of industrialists, 'that the very fact that he (the African) is forced into squatting has often created the need for a Bantu to have his family with him so that his wife can look after him.'[6] Hostels, he said, would make this unnecessary. 'If he lives in single quarters he can very often save much more for his family and his future. The chance of his family progressing and his children being well trained is much greater in his home area than under those terrible conditions in which such families very often have to live when they move into the neighbourhood of a city.'[7]

The following year the Department of Native Affairs issued the further directive that when African family housing was absolutely necessary, it would have to be designed in such a way as to be convertible at a later stage to singles' quarters and then finally to coloured housing, when the Africans had all left. The houses were thus constructed in long rows with connecting walls which could be knocked down or put up during each new phase of apartheid.

WINDERMERE

The government began the removal programme in the shanty

72

towns. The oldest and largest camp was Windermere, built behind the industrial suburb of Maitland. Coloureds were first segregated from Africans and sent to new exclusively coloured townships on the Cape Flats. The 2 500 African families were then screened according to Section 10 of the new Urban Areas Act. Seven hundred and fifty families qualified as '10 (1a's)' or '10 (1b's)'. They were resettled in another squatter camp twelve miles away which was gradually turned into a brick township. Twelve hundred families were ordered to separate — husbands to the hostels, wives and children up country. The authorities could not sort out the remaining 500 families easily and so ordered them to dismantle their shacks and re-erect them at 'Nyanga Emergency Camp' where squatters from all thirty camps in the city were being herded. There the families were told to wait until they were either assigned homes or repatriated.

'Nyanga Emergency Camp' was visited in July 1956 by a contributor to *South African Outlook*.[8] The shanty town, he said, was well out of sight from the main roads. The ground had not been levelled. 'Each family had erected its own shack (if it could) on the top, or on the sloping side, of a sand dune, so as to keep out of the wet.'

As the man entered the camp, he saw a truck arriving with a family, its chickens, and all its belongings. 'I watched the offloading; and then the mother, a frail-looking woman with three very small children, stood watching her husband, with one other man, rapidly trying with a few very old pieces of corrugated iron, to knock up some sort of shelter for the night.'

The first bitter accounts of families driven from Cape Town began with the 'sorting out' of Windermere and the other 'black spots' on the Cape Flats. Myrna Blumberg, a reporter for the liberal white newspaper *Contact*, met Eddie Tembani in a section of Windermere called Strongyard.[9] He was a sixty-year-old van driver who had been in Cape Town for several years but had been hospitalized several times for tuberculosis. He thus did not qualify as a '10 (1b)' because he had not worked in one firm for ten consecutive years. 'Now they say forget your wife, forget your baby. Go and be a bachelor.'

Blumberg also spoke with Sam Mbaba, a factory worker, as he pulled down his shack on a mud path called Fourteenth Avenue. Mbaba's wife and children had been 'endorsed out' to Oudtshoorn, 300 miles away in the Eastern Cape, and he had been assigned a bunk in the bachelors' quarters. So many families were torn apart during the removals that the Institute of Race Relations established an advice office to help all those with pass problems. The following accounts, culled from the Institute's files, are striking in their similarity to the stories told by the Modderdam squatters twenty years later.[10]

'B C came to Cape Town about fifteen years ago to marry J C, who had regular employment there. They had four children. Early in 1959 the husband died, and when B C went to renew her residential permit she was told that she must return to the Reserves to join her husband's people. Although she protested that his only relative was a married brother with whom he had been on very bad terms, the authorities insisted that she must go, and threatened to pull down her small dwelling in Windermere. After protracted representations by the Institute of Race Relations they relented to the extent of allowing her to remain as a domestic servant, resident on her employer's premises. The four children, however, who ranged between ten months and seven years in age, had to be sent home to her parents in a Reserve. As a result of all this worry, she became very ill with a nervous complaint, and was forced to go to stay with her mother in an area where there are no means of reasonable subsistence.'

'Mrs E C, who was 8½ months pregnant, came with her two small children to the office of the Institute of Race Relations for assistance in getting her residential permit renewed. She was provided with a letter to the Manager of Native Administration. She had not proceeded more than ten yards, on leaving the office, when she was arrested, she and the children being roughly bundled into a police van . . . After much investigation the Institute traced her and persuaded the magistrate to have her sent to hospital immediately. The other children were kept at the hospital which was able to get in touch with a relative, who took them in pending the mother's discharge from hospital.'

'Mrs M S came to Cape Town in 1941, when she was a child, and later married W B by customary rites. In 1955, after her children had died, he turned her out and took another wife. She worked and saved money to obtain a small pondok in which to live. When her brother died in 1957 she went to his home in Burghersdorp for the funeral and remained there for three months (the only break in her residence in Cape Town) returning with two of her brother's children whom she took as wards. As a result of

74

this short break she was repeatedly arrested, on the third occasion being sentenced to £8 or 40 days. She had no money by this time, so was forced to serve the sentence, but became seriously ill in jail and ultimately was released when friends paid £3 on her behalf. Three days later she was again arrested, given a suspended sentence, and warned to leave the area and to pull down her pondok. She demolished it as ordered, left her possessions lying in the road and her wards with friends, and came to the Institute for help. She had no home in the Reserves to which she could go, and all her relatives were in Cape Town. Ultimately, after much negotiation, the authorities permitted her to stay and to share a house with another family.'

MORE HOSTELS

Most of the squatter camps around Cape Town were dismantled by 1960, the year Eiselen retired. More than ten thousand women had been sent home and many thousands more were arrested for pass violations. Yet despite the government's energetic work, the African population of Cape Town had grown once again from 100 000 to 180 000.

A new campaign to revive the removal scheme was launched in 1962. A National Party study group published a report reviewing the history of the Eiselen line and called on the government to step up the programme. *Die Burger,* the official National Party newspaper in the Cape supported the cry. In a series of editorials, it linked the scheme explicitly to the success of apartheid or 'separate development' throughout the country. 'If ... the Western Cape cannot be an example of the disintegration of Bantu labour, then we must indeed begin to ask ourselves if the National policy of separate development for the Bantu is in any way capable of practical application.'[11]

Two months later, the paper went even further: 'The Western Cape must be the pioneer. It must be the symbol.' For this reason, the paper said, the removal scheme must be publicized extensively. 'It must be made unmistakeably clear that the party's policy is being carried out. But naturally not only in the Western Cape. *The policy is designed for South Africa as a whole* ... '[12] [Emphasis added.]

Die Transvaler, the Johannesburg National Party newspaper, made the same argument. 'What is being planned in miniature for the Western Cape is the government's policy also for the rest of the Republic.'[13] The removal plan, the paper said, was an opportunity to try out methods of removing African labour which would later be necessary 'for the greater task in which some millions will be involved.'

During this newspaper campaign, *Die Burger* gave prominence to reports that some Afrikaner businessmen and farmers were willing to reduce the number of their African employees. The Afrikaanse Sakekamer (Chamber of Commerce) met on August 8 to discuss the plan. 'If whites cannot remove the Bantu from the Western Cape, our apartheid policy will never succeed,' Dr P E Bissenbach said. He went on to counter economic arguments against the scheme. 'Sacrifices will have to be made. When we voted for apartheid, we also voted for sacrifices.'[14]

The paper also printed an article by a member of parliament, Mr F S Steyn, who saw the scheme as a means for providing a last line of defence for white South Africa. By removing the Bantu from the Western Cape, he said, about 37 percent of the total area of the Republic would be free of Africans. 'This would provide a permanent White bastion and would give a geographical content to the policy of separate development.'[15]

Verwoerd endorsed the revived programme later that month. 'The government is determined to proceed with the removal of the Bantu from the Western Cape . . . In ten years time we will look back and say that what was done then was well and properly done.'[16] He established three committees to study and implement the removal plans. The Department of Coloured Affairs also set up local committees to assist in the substitution of coloured workers for Africans. Their task, however, was formidable for the African work force was over 100 000 but less than 500 coloureds were listed as unemployed. Enthusiasm for the project was high nonetheless. There was a suggestion to import Eastern Cape coloureds to the Western Cape. The government-owned railways recruited stevedores from amongst the small coloured population in the Transkei in order to replace Xhosas from the same region who had been in the docks for years. Farmers relied increasingly on prison labour. Thirteen farm jails had been built in the region during the late forties. They provided 2 000 workers — many of whom, ironically, had been convicted of being in the Western Cape illegally.

Yet even these measures could not reduce the size of the African work force. In the two years which followed the new campaign, the population increased again. Almost 1 500 men and over 2 500 women were endorsed out in 1962, but close to 4 000 men were brought in on contract. In the first three months of 1964, four thousand more were hired.

The transformation of settled African workers back into a class of migrants was written into law during 1964. A further amendment to the Native Urban Areas Act denied rural African men the right to seek work in Cape Town. They were only allowed to stay in the city for more than 72 hours if they had already been issued a contract up country. As contract workers, they could never win residence rights in the city. For although their contracts could be renewed annually during their mandatory trip to their old village, this broke their continuous residence in the city and barred them from winning '10 (1b)' rights. This new class of workers was appropriately called 'permanent temporaries'.

The bill also prohibited women from obtaining contracts, and abolished a previous ruling which enabled a family to join a father or husband in Cape Town if there was sufficient accommodation. No legal means thus remained for a woman from outside the city to spend more than three days in Cape Town. Mr S F Froneman, a member of Parliament who served on the Bantu Affairs Commission, supported the legislation by echoing once again the cry for 'white cities' which had been heard twenty, forty and sixty years earlier. 'This bill contains one single principle, namely that the Bantu in the white areas constitute only a temporary labour force and not a permanent part of the white population.'[17] Soon after, the government announced plans to reduce the African population by five percent annually.

The full impact of the removal scheme became clear twenty years after it was announced. Between 1951 and 1953, there was an average of three men in Langa to every woman. In 1970, there were ten men to one woman. Of almost 25 000 men living legally in the township, less than 3 000 lived with their families. In Nyanga there were almost nine thousand men and two thousand women. Only in Guguletu was the number of men and women roughly equivalent.

During the same period, the number of pass arrests had grown to over 30 000 from 1 000. There were no contract workers in Cape Town in the early fifties. By 1970, 42 percent of the total African work force was on contract. Eighty-five percent of all male Africans lived in single quarters and new hostels were being planned for 24 000 more men.

The effect of the scheme on the rural areas was far more grim. In the mid-seventies, a statistical study of migrants in Cape Town was made which showed the extent to which areas in the Transkei and Ciskei had deteriorated in the fifty years since James Henderson had reported gross poverty in the land.[18] Of two hundred people interviewed in the camps and hostels of Cape Town, 43 percent had no land in the 'homelands' at all. Seventy-eight percent had less than five acres. Those who had land to plough grew an average of six bags in a normal year, which in 1975 could be sold for a total of R40. Forty-six percent owned no cattle, 50 percent had no sheep, 64 percent had no goats, 71 percent had no pigs, and 61 percent had no more than one chicken. Seventy percent spent only three weeks or a month each year in the homelands. Many who stayed longer said they did so not to farm or relax, but because they could not get a contract to return sooner.

The researchers concluded, 'No less than 26 percent of the families produced no income at all and are therefore completely landless. (They are effectively a rural proletariat.) More than half of the families produced less than R8 per month, while more than three-quarters made R24 or less.'[19]

The migrants in Cape Town made an average of R23 per week, of which they sent home an average of R11 per month, an amount which depended on how many men sent home money to more than one family. Thus a woman up country with three children under fifteen who was fortunate enough to produce R10 of food each month, might receive R30 or R40 from her husband, brothers and other relatives. This is not enough to survive. For in 1975, the monthly cost of clothing, fuel and light, cleansing and toilet articles, transport, tax, housing maintenance and religious rituals for one month was forty rand. And even without paying for education (R7 per month), it cost fifteen rand to keep a child from ten to fifteen healthy, R12 for one aged five to nine, and eight rand for a child under the age of four. Thus to raise and educate her children and feed herself for one month, a country woman would need about R100 — more than twice her income. The only place she could find extra money was in the city, where her husband's monthly wages averaged R100.

Verwoerd had predicted that the redevelopment of the migrant system would both help the villager save, and reduce the African pressure on the city. Instead the 'model plan' for apartheid only made the demand to come to Cape Town more desperate than ever before.

PART 3
The Campaign

7. Bush Crashing

The return of thousands of Africans to Cape Town began ten years after the government resolved to reduce their numbers in the Western Cape by five percent annually; fifteen years after the squatter camps were first dismantled; twenty years after the removal scheme was announced; and twenty-five years after the National Party came to power, pledging to stop the African influx to the city.

The new immigrants were refugees from the very hostels, villages and resettlement camps in which the government had hoped to contain them. Their presence was both a powerful refutation of apartheid and proof that no government could stop the movement of Africans into the city. The squatters threatened to overturn the pass laws, damage the migrant labour system and make a mockery of Eiselen's removal scheme.

The anti-squatter campaign escalated in the seventies. Official brutality was increasingly justified in Parliament and in the press by the old homilies of white rule. Shacks were burnt, pregnant women deported, and families pulled apart, it was claimed, because African workers were in the cities temporarily. Their families had to stay in the villages in order that the worker would remain 'good'.

The shanties of the squatters revealed the bankruptcy of the government's ideology, to which it nonetheless clung with intensity.

WERKGENOT

Werkgenot, a mile from where Modderdam was later built, was one of the new camps. About 100 shanties teetered over a brackish pond unknown to almost everyone in Cape Town except the squatters themselves. Marius de Jager, an employee of the municipality of Bellville, had become aware of the camp during the winter of 1974.[1] He was, he said, often assigned 'to track down squatters and make reports.' On October 21, he received a call from Mr W F Coetzee of the Bantu Affairs Administration Board, who asked him to arrange that Werkgenot be bulldozed on the night of October 25. City engineer John Marshall, Mr De Jager's boss, approved Mr Coetzee's request and told the bulldozer driver, Cornelius Goosen, to go along as well.

Mr De Jager and two BAAB officials parked their cars behind the factories off Modderdam Road a day before the raid, and walked around the pond over the small sand dunes to the camp. Speaking Afrikaans, they told a few men who had not gone to work that the bulldozer would arrive the next day. Only twenty percent of the residents spoke Afrikaans, Mr De Jager said, but those who did assured the officials that they would tell their neighbours.

Mr G J Niewoudt, a mechanic for the Bellville municipality, was awakened at 3.00 a.m. on the warm spring morning of October 26 by the rumble of the town's bulldozer which was kept in his yard. He ran outside and found Mr Goosen warming up the engine. Mr Niewoudt, who had heard that 'certain operations were being planned' for that night, decided to follow Mr Goosen in his own car 'out of curiosity'. The two men set off in convoy for Werkgenot.

They found the operation already in progress when they arrived. Five Bantu Administration officials were on hand — Mr Coetzee, Mr Douglas Johnson, Mr Peter du Toit, Mr Clarence Moller, Mr Johannes Lourens — as well as a contingent of seven policemen headed by Sergeant I J Brand. The raid was being carried out 'like a military exercise' according to Mr Johnson. One group of policemen stood guard at the edges of the camp to make sure no squatters escaped into the bush, while the rest began a house-to-house search for 'illegal Bantu'.

The squatters were screaming. Mrs Janet Nyilimani wrapped herself in a blanket and hurried next door where she found her neighbour in labour. Mr Pepe Vetani was getting dressed when something hit him on the ankle. He fell to the ground, then hopped to his house. Mr Ncinci Vuvane, who also heard the shouting, went outside and was grabbed by a policeman who first

81

demanded his reference book and then threw him into a police van. Several shanties were set on fire as the bulldozer began to knock down the shacks. Mr Vetani saw two officials with plastic bottles of methyl alcohol in their hands. 'They were coming to set the house alight. I saw them asking the people standing next to the pondokkie that was next to mine for matches.' Mrs Nelson Jilaji and Mr Albert Shume said they saw Mr Lourens throw 'spirits' over their houses and set them on fire.

According to Mr du Toit, however, only Mr De Jager was responsible for setting shacks on fire. He yelled at one woman repeatedly, telling her to pack up quickly because he was anxious to knock her shack down. 'Several times he told her to hurry. She was still busy packing the things when he said to me, "I will show them, I will just set one or two of these pondoks alight." ' Mr du Toit then saw Mr De Jager squirting the 'spirits' onto a shack. Mr Moller said he also saw Mr De Jager walk into a shanty with an open bottle. 'I saw a sprinkling motion with his hand . . . I saw him strike a match and then put the upper half of his body into the pondok which caught alight.' Mr De Jager admitted to causing the two fires, but said that he had done so to create a firebreak to keep the flames from spreading to a third shanty. He believed that the original fire had been caused by accident. 'I suspect a candle or something must have fallen over in that hut.'

As the squatters groped frantically for their possessions amid the flames and the bulldozer crashed through the shacks, the officials relaxed and played games. Sergeant Brand 'bushcrashed' his landrover over the sand dunes. Two of the BAAB officials sat down for coffee while the three others threw bottles and sticks at the squatters' chickens. Mr Niewoudt, who watched these antics, said the officials were 'full of sport and boisterous. I'm not prepared to say they were drunk, but they were obviously under the influence.'

Mr De Jager and Mr Goosen knocked down shanties until sunrise, at which time they left 'to do more important work fixing pavements.' A few of the shacks were left standing but were demolished during the following two weeks. Several of the squatters lost all their possessions. Mr Vuvane returned to the camp when he was released from prison and found his house burnt, with nothing left but the iron frame of an alarm clock. Mr Jilaji lost his minibus which he used for business, as well as his house and everything inside it. Mr and Mrs Sam Tshepe lost their

Modderdam from the air. photo, The Cape Times

photos, Gavin Younge

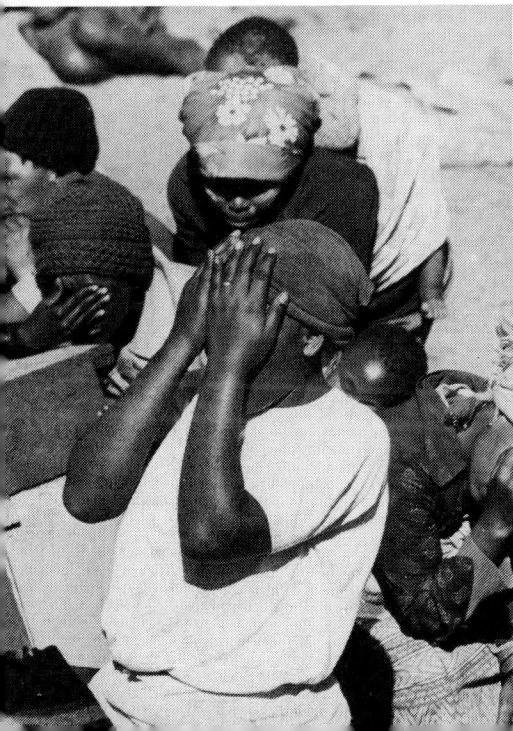

photos, The Argus

photos, Gavin You

home which they had built for R48. Other squatters charged that the officials had stolen money hidden under mattresses when they ransacked the shanties.

Despite the participation of the police and other officials, the raid had no legal foundation. Under the Prevention of Illegal Squatting Act, 1951, a shanty could not be destroyed without a court order or the permission of the landowner. Furthermore, a squatter's property could not be damaged in the demolition even if a court order was obtained. Mr Vetani, Mr Vuvani, Mr and Mrs Jilaji all brought charges against Mr De Jager and Mr Goosen for malicious damage to property. The details of the raid emerged during the trial.

CROSSROADS

The number of court cases increased with the number of squatters. The suits were brought through the financial and legal assistance of the Institute of Race Relations and other white liberal organizations. About twenty shanties were erected near Nyanga township during February, 1975. Several had been put up by former residents of Werkgenot. Several hundred additional families settled in over the Easter weekend. By mid-April there were over 1 000 shacks and almost 4 000 people. Many of the Africans said they had been sent to the camp by officials who had evicted them from the legal coloured shanty towns. Mr Fanie Botha, the local Bantu Affairs Commissioner, denied their claims. Most of the squatters, he said, are 'illegally present in the Western Cape and do not qualify for family housing within the area.'[2]

The first raid on the new camp, which had been called Crossroads, began at 5.00 a.m., on May 2. Thirty-four squatters were arrested for pass offences and for trespassing. As they drove off with their prisoners, the officials warned of future raids. During the next few months, selected shanties were knocked down and many women were arrested while their husbands were at work. Finally two squatters brought a suit against the Board for destruction of property. In court, the lawyer for the two people led evidence that the Board neither had permission to knock down the shanties nor owned the land, as it had claimed. The judge ruled on the side of the squatters. He issued a restraining order prohibiting the demolition of any occupied shacks. He also delivered an angry lecture to the officials. Squatters, he said, had so little protection that it was important to respect and observe strictly what they *did* have.

The Board did not contest the ruling, but harassed the squatters with continual pass raids and badgered women into signing papers they could not read which authorized the dismantling of their own shacks. Over 1 000 arrests were made and about eighty women were returned to rural areas.

Mr Thabatha had worked in Cape Town for thirty years, but his wife, Jane, had been refused permission to stay permanently.[3] Mrs Thabatha was eight months pregnant when she was first visited by BAAB officials. They allowed her to remain in the city until the child was born and old enough to travel. She gave birth to a boy through Caesarian section shortly afterwards in Groote Schuur Hospital and returned to Crossroads to recuperate. While Mr Thabatha was at work one morning in October, the officials returned. She was told to leave behind those possessions she could not carry and was driven to the station with two of her children and put onto a train bound for the Transkei. She got off at Worcester, three hours away, switched trains, and came back to Cape Town.

The officials discovered her a month later. When Mr Thabatha came home from work that day, his wife and children had been deported a second time and his house had been bulldozed. He received a letter from Mrs Thabatha a few days later describing the terrible journey. She also complained that she had not received any of the possessions from their shack that were to have gone with her on the train. Mr Thabatha was unable to trace his two new beds, radio, bank books, blankets, or anything else, although Board officials referred him to a house in Guguletu where they thought they might be stored. Mr Thabatha said 'I had always thought that Whites show great respect for their women, and that they would show the same for ours.'

Brig. Jan van der Westhuizen of the Bantu Affairs Administrative Board defended the Board's actions and charged that it was the white liberals who were really to blame. In a letter to *Die Burger*,[4] he argued: 'A large number of the people were willing to leave after the first cases in court and those held before the Bantu Affairs Commissioner. Through certain people, however, advice was given to the residents and this was spread widely among them. After this, they all refused to move, despite the suspended sentences.

As a result, each one must now be physically removed.' Van der Westhuizen then defended the migrant labour system. 'Family life was broken when these men came to the city the first time to work without their families. It did not happen now suddenly, when the Board sent them back.'

The harassment of the Crossroads squatters ceased without explanation in December 1975. While the residents hoped that BAAB had had a change of heart or policy, they suspected that the lull in arrests was evidence of pending legislation which would reduce the squatters' legal protection.

IN PARLIAMENT

The squatters' fears were justified. The proposed new law, the Prevention of Illegal Squatting Amendment Act, 1976, was tabled during the next session of Parliament. No longer would a court order be needed to dismantle a shack. Instead, BAAB, or any other local body, could simply post an eviction notice seven days before the demolition. Furthermore, no landowner could allow squatters on his land without government approval and an employer was barred from hiring a black without legal accommodation.

The tabling of the Bill led to yet another recapitulation of the long debate on black urbanization. The National Party, now with a majority of 92 in the House of Assembly, clung to their stand that Africans were in the cities temporarily and that harsher pass laws were the solution to squatting. They also resurrected the vision of white cities besieged by blacks (a decisive factor in the election of 1948.)

The opposition, now split between the United Party and the more aggressive Progressive-Reform Party, had 38 seats altogether. They argued in vain as they had done for thirty years, that it was impossible to keep blacks out of the cities.

The Minister of Community Development, Marais Steyn, opened the debate. He accused white liberals of defending the squatters when they defied the new law. The law, he said, had to be changed because of the squatters' court victories. 'If it were possible to dispose of the normal legal procedures,' he said, 'I would prefer — I can assure honourable members of this — to comply with those procedures but I am afraid that in view of the unavoidable delays with such procedures, we would not be able to deal with the problem effectively.'[5]

Nationalist MP A van Breda then attacked the squatters themselves. It was not economics but subversive politics which brought them to town, he said. 'There is a special system of communication between squatters and aspirant squatters,' he cried as opposition members tried to hoot him down. Through this 'bush telegraph', he claimed, men and women learned about the deficiencies of the old squatter law and therefore flocked in their thousands to the city.

Furthermore, he charged, most of the squatters didn't want to work anyway. 'It is really an undeniable truth that a considerable percentage of the squatter families who cannot be housed due to economic reasons fall into a category which is not able to comply with socially accepted norms. In other words, they are people who do not want to live under better conditions than squatting conditions.'

As the debate wore on, the criticism of the squatters became more and more outraged. Mr J P A Reyneke said the new law was necessary to teach the squatters a lesson. 'This problem of squatting involves responsibility, a sense of responsibility which we must cultivate, and which is lacking among those squatters who simply trek.' Mr Reyneke argued that the major cause of shanty towns was 'the irresponsible behaviour of the head of the family.'

'Possibly one can simply teach some of these people a lesson from nature and the animal kingdom. What bird does not first build its nest so that the little ones which are hatched will at least have protection and safety? Therefore it is also time for us to teach these squatters responsibility and also discipline to a certain degree.'

It was Mr J T Albertyn, however, who tied the squatter problem directly to the requirements of the migrant labour system. 'The Bantu who is here legally concluded an agreement when he was recruited as a labourer in the White area, that he would come here as a single person for a certain period of time and under certain conditions. He accepted that agreement, and now, in spite of that agreement, he brings his wife and children here illegally. He moves out of the accommodation with which he is provided and which is being paid for in any event, and goes and squats at Crossroads and other places.' Therefore, Mr Albertyn argued, the government had the right to take any measure it wished against the squatters. 'I want to ask a question: — What moral claim does such a person have on society if he gives up his home and job and simply comes and squats in another area where he is not allowed to be? What does society owe these people? I do not believe society owes them anything at all. By squatting, they are living off society as parasites.'

The opposition attacked the Bill with sarcasm and exasperation, reiterating the argument which had been made since the turn of the century that the creation of a settled black proletariat in Cape Town and throughout South Africa was inevitable and that all measures which attempted to deny this — from influx control to the Eiselen Plan to the Squatter Bill under debate — would inevitably fail.

Dr Van Zyl Slabbert, a former sociology lecturer at the University of Cape Town, and later the leader of the opposition, provided the most complete analysis. He said that if Parliament wanted to conduct a fruitful debate on squatting, it was necessary to see the phenomenon in the broader context of industrialization. 'The reason is that it is a symptom of unequal economic growth. There are stronger growth points in the urban areas, whereas the rural areas are unable to accommodate the surplus labour.' This imbalance, he said, was compounded by population growth. Thirdly, he explained, migration patterns were distorted. 'It is cases of over-urbanization that make it necessary for large-scale unproductive capital expenditure to be incurred in the short term in order to provide housing and basic services. These are processes, factors, which are operating in our society and in any other society in Africa. That is why we are going to have to contend with squatting in the future.'

He then defended the squatters in their own words. 'The women say that they come with their children to stay with their husbands. The men say that they are unable to find accommodation for themselves and also, on top of that, provide for their wives in the Transkei. The wives say that there is no work in the Transkei. The government now says that the women and children must return to the Transkei and the men to their single quarters in the areas where they live. However, the women and children refuse to return. That is how simple the situation is.'

The debate continued throughout the week. It became evident that the law would not only be devastating for African squatters but would further divide Africans and coloureds — for while Africans faced banishment to hostels and homelands, coloured squatters were promised new housing around Cape Town. Shortly before the vote was taken, however, Mr Steyn denied that the hardships facing African squatters were too great. There were, he said with annoyance, still places for them to live if they returned to the rural areas. 'They are not spirits from another world who manifest themselves as adults among us. Surely they come from somewhere. We hope this measure will deter them from coming to Cape Town while they have neither housing nor families with whom they can be temporarily housed. We hope that, as a result of this measure, they will preferably decide to stay where they are . . . After all, they are making a living at the moment.'

The Prevention of Illegal Squatting Amendment Act 1976 was passed by a vote of 92 to 42.

MODDERDAM

Shacks were being constructed off Modderdam Road as Parliament debated. Although some squatters had been in the bushes for as long as two years, it was only in May that new shacks were visible from the road. The camp soon became a test of the government's renewed squatter war.

Mr Isaac Nkondo, one of the camp's pioneers, told me of its founding.

'At first there were just fifteen families. We hid from the outside world. We used to put some leaves on the roofs of the houses, because we were near the airport. We advised people to put some tree branches on the footpaths so that footprints could not be traced. We left the camp early in the morning when it was still dark and came back after the sun set to avoid being detected by cops or officials. We used to enter the bush one by one and stand by the road to look to see if anyone was watching us. Then we would slip into the bushes as if to pass water. We bought our wives dogs to protect them from the skollies but we had to be careful that the dogs did not make noise and attract people.'

The Nkondos stayed quietly in the same shack for almost two years. Then in late 1975 they learned that houses would soon be built on the land.

'The inspectors came around to evict us and we did not know where we could go next. But one of the coloured men who was working with the whites took us aside and whispered that no houses were going to be built across the tracks. He thought we would be safe if we stayed well hidden. We were getting ready to move when the bulldozers came one night and crushed all our zincs. They made a hole in the ground and threw them in and said, 'If you want them, you know where to find them.'

Mr Nkondo had paid R100 for the material. When he and his family moved to the new ground, a quarter of mile away, he could only afford a cardboard shack covered with a plastic tarp.

'We stayed like this for four months. We wondered how long we could keep hidden as we were now nearer the road and people were coming in and out so often. Then they started chasing people from another camp. People were given train tickets which were good only for half the trip home. After that the people had to pay. They said, 'This is *too* much.' So within a few weeks, more than a hundred shacks were put up. You could see them from the road. It was impossible to hide anymore. But in a way we felt safer because we thought that there were too many people to be moved easily.'

Bushes were cut and burned and paths became big enough for trucks and cars to bring in furniture and zincs.

Mr Nkondo decided it was time to build a better shack and went out to a scrap yard and brought back the new walls, roof and floor in a hired van. The new house was up in a day. 'No one really knew what was going to happen. The police saw us here and we did not know when they might start arresting for passes or try to knock it all down.'

The first heavy rain of the winter fell during the night of June 2. Water streamed so quickly through gullies in the sand that some of the squatters whose homes were on lower ground were spending the night with their drier neighbours. The Nkondos were awakened by shouts and screams at 11.30 p.m. Police were pounding on the doors of the shanties, demanding passes. Mr Nkondo ran outside. The camp was alive with darting flashlight beams. Mr Nkondo saw several women being herded by policemen wearing heavy raincoats and long rubber boots to a wagon parked in the bush. He slipped back into his shack, and told his wife to take the blankets and hide with their daughter in the bush. He grabbed his knobkerrie and joined about thirty other squatters who were also armed with clubs, pick handles and stones. They quickly surrounded three policemen standing apart from the rest. Someone whacked one of the policemen in the mouth and he stumbled and fell. The other policemen's legs were flailed until they, too, were on the ground. Their friends came to their rescue by firing in the air and storming the crowd.

The battle lasted for almost half an hour. David Crawage, a student at the University of the Western Cape, was driving his 10-speed bicycle back to campus when he heard shooting. He peddled into the mob, and when he was dragged out by a policeman, his face was lacerated and it appeared as though his skull was fractured. Mr W Josephs was driving home from a cookingware demonstration and stopped along Modderdam Road when he saw the police vans. 'It was an incredible sight. I had to keep moving and count myself lucky to still be in one piece.'[6]

The squatters retreated into the bush shortly after midnight. Mr Nkondo found his wife and child safe, huddled together to stay warm. The family joined other squatters along Modderdam Road an hour later. They chanted hymns and stoned passing cars. Police sealed off the road by 1.00 a.m. and the squatters gradually returned to their shacks. It was still raining.

The *Cape Times* reported the next day that about 30 squatters had been arrested for passes and that Mr Crawage and two policemen were hospitalized. The raid had taken place only weeks after the Prevention of Illegal Squatting Amendment Bill had been passed. Rev. Louis Banks of the Western Province Council of Churches called the incident 'a direct outgrowth of the law.'[7] Bantu Administration Board official Mr A McLachlan, however, denied that they had entered the camp to evict the squatters. He said they were simply there 'to investigate the presence of Bantu people illegally in the Cape' and that they had come at night because that was the only time when squatters could be found at home. He did not know how long the camp had been in existence. But, he said, the Board had received 'plenty of complaints from coloured and white residents in Bellville about thieves staying in the area.'

8. The Student Revolt

The story of Modderdam now shifts to the black areas surrounding the camp. By the early 1970s, the impact of the long years of apartheid, pass laws and the Eiselen plan was as severe in the cities as in the bush. The government's schemes had not only created a class of rural Africans forced into the city to survive, but had also made increasingly desperate the plight of those with rights to live in town.

Two groups had grown up in the African townships whose immediate needs and ambitions were directly opposed. At one pole were the students, whose parents had come to the shanty towns of Windermere, Cook's Bush and other camps built in the 1940s and 1950s. All they knew of the rural areas was what they might have learned from their parents or from visits to relatives. But because they grew up during the years of the removal scheme, they had been pushed by the government throughout their lives to abandon the city for the Ciskei and the Transkei. They were required to study agriculture in school. If they were absent from Cape Town for six months, they could lose their '10 (1a)' rights, be endorsed out to the homelands, and allowed to return to their homes only after a year in Cape Town. They faced expulsion even if they were unable to find a job. Yet the 'coloured first' employment policy under the Eiselen Plan excluded even the best educated Africans from all but the most menial jobs. High school graduates remained unemployed or worked for R25 a week in factories or railway stations. The students were thus afraid to leave Cape Town, yet had little prospect of a better home or working conditions than those of their parents. Unmarried, they had little to lose by rebelling.

At the other extreme were the migrants, who comprised over half the population of the African townships. Although they were hit as hard by the same laws which restricted the students, they stood to lose the little they did have in a revolt. Their claim on the city was already so precarious that any disruption could easily result in their deportation. There were many more men waiting up country to replace them after their yearly contract expired. Furthermore, many of them justified their lives in the hostels by keeping their land in the village. If they lost their jobs, all the years of loneliness would have been wasted.

The fears of both students and migrants intensified in the mid-seventies with the announcement that the Transkei was to be granted independence, and that Xhosa speakers both up country and in Cape Town would be given passports in place of their passes — thus further weakening their hold on the city. The students feared that if they acquiesced, eventually they would be driven from the city. The migrants believed that their chance to survive in Cape Town depended on their ability to keep quiet and continue working.

These tensions broke during the winter of 1976. They were sparked off by the uprising in the Johannesburg township of Soweto which, in turn, was prompted by police disruption of a demonstration against the use of Afrikaans in schools as a medium of instruction. First Africans then coloureds were in revolt in Cape Town for five months. The revolt in the city had two main phases. The first, which lasted from August to the middle of September, was directed at white institutions inside and outside the township. These demonstrations, burnings, and pitched battles with riot squads in army fatigue, culminated in marches through the centre of Cape Town and a city-wide 'stay-away'. The second phase, which lasted until the end of the year, was led by African students against those blacks within the townships regarded as opportunists or collaborators.

The full story of the Cape Town uprising is beyond the scope of this book. Here I have focused on only one aspect of the revolt — the deepening and ultimately violent split between the students and the migrants. This division had an immense impact on the people of Modderdam and showed how the efforts to stop the growth of an African working class had evolved over thirty years into an effective method of suppressing black rebellion.

SOWETO

Two weeks after the police raid on Modderdam, the revolt began in the Orlando section of Soweto, near the place where Mpanza had led his first squatter movement thirty-two years earlier.

As it spread to black townships east of Johannesburg, to Pretoria and rural towns several hundred miles away, the official death toll reached 176 at the week's end. Private sources believed it to be much higher. Except for two white officials, the others killed on the first day were blacks. Sixty-seven beer halls and bottle stores were burned, as well as 53 BAAB offices, 84 post offices and hundreds of cars, trucks and buses.

In Cape Town, riot police dispersed a crowd of Africans who had surrounded the car of a government official outside the Langa BAAB office on June 24. Neither teargas nor bullets were used, but the tension built up nonetheless throughout black Cape Town. 'You could just feel it,' a resident of Guguletu said. 'You woke up each morning wanting to know if this was the day. When you walked outside, everything was too still. We didn't know where or when, but we knew this thing was coming for sure.'

Students brought newspapers and transistor radios into the school yards. 'They interrupted lessons,' one teacher recalled. 'They would jump up and say, "Now we must talk about Soweto." ' On the morning of August 11, students came into his class more agitated than they had been since the first reports of the uprising. The class began to sing 'Nkosi Sikelel' iAfrika', the African National Anthem. A student ran into the classroom at about 10.30 and shouted, 'They've started at Langa.' Everyone rose from their desks and gathered on the playing field. They marched with clenched fists onto NY I, the main road of Guguletu, directly into the police lines. At the end of the day, the official death toll — again widely disputed — stood at nineteen. All were black.

During the next weeks, the African students would gather each morning in school yards to choose the day's targets. 'We had no leader,' one student said. 'We would just gather in a crowd. Someone would shout, "Let's hit so-and-so." Someone else would name another place. Then a few people would run one way and everyone would follow.'

The African rebellion was preceded by two weeks by demonstrations and boycotts at the University of the Western Cape — the centre of coloured resistance in Cape Town. Classes were picketed, an administration building was burned, and when one of the student leaders was detained, students lined Modderdam Road pelting police vans and passing cars with rocks.

The demonstrations continued throughout the first days of the fighting in Langa. By the end of August coloured high school students had also joined in the rebellion. The poorest coloured townships, Bonteheuwel, Mannenburg and Hanover Park became battlefields and at least thirty-three blacks died.

This phase of the rebellion culminated the first week in September in brief marches by coloured and African students through the centre of Cape Town. The success of these demonstrations led the students to call for a general strike. Pamphlets were distributed: 'STAY AT HOME, SHOW YOUR SUPPORT FOR THE STUDENTS. HIT THE SYSTEM WHERE IT HURTS.' Despite rumours of a last minute postponement, 60 percent of the coloured and African work force stayed home on September 15 and over 70 percent were absent the next day. The students, it seemed, had briefly established unity between themselves and the black working classes, something the government had been trying to prevent for so long.

The only group within the township which resisted both the calls to support the revolt and the strike were the migrants. Precluded from the life of the township and the city for years, they simply could not afford to risk losing their jobs. The longer the rebellion continued, the more it appeared to threaten their own life struggle for some independence from white control. In the first days of the uprising, a construction manager told a reporter that despite the turmoil, the migrants were still coming to work. His remarks closely echoed those of labour recruiters sixty years ago who favoured the 'raw untutored Native' who wanted only to do a job and go home. 'Our black workers come to us from the Transkei and all they are concerned with is doing a job and earning money. The last thing they want to do is to fight and cause trouble. In spite of being threatened by youngsters, they have all been turning up for work.'[1]

The strike calls confirmed the migrants' worst fears. As employers talked about firing those who honoured the stay-away, the migrants saw that there was little in the rebellion for them. 'I once didn't go to work when I was being cheated on my wages,' one contract worker told me. 'But I did not see how it would help me as long as I was getting paid. None of the students ever came to tell us what we were to do if we lost our jobs.'

The revolt came to a peak with the strike and the weekend of violence which followed it. Workers returned to their jobs and the coloured students drifted back to school. In the African townships, however, the students struggled to sustain the momentum of the revolt by shifting targets. With hundreds of their friends dead, imprisoned, or in exile and with the schools, government offices and other symbols of white authority destroyed, the students attempted to strengthen their leadership by radicalizing or 'conscientizing' the townships. The students were also anxious to punish those who had not supported them. This campaign had great success initially, but the students made a fatal mistake — they did not consider the special problems of the migrants. As the 'conscientization' campaign built up, the rift between the students and the migrants became ugly.

After having fought the police, the students no longer hesitated to use force. One October night, a group of eight students called at the home of an African businessman who had worn a police uniform during the fighting, and had told the press that the students were only 'thieves and hoodlums'. When the students broke the lock, they found an old man sitting alone in the house. They asked him to identify his clothes and other belongings, quickly carried them out of the house and piled them on the pavement. They told the man to get out and then hurled Molotov cocktails through a window.

The students' main targets were the shebeens. They left notes under the doors of the shebeen owners, ordering them to close in mourning for the riot dead. During the weekend of October 22, the students broke into almost all those which remained open, fighting with customers and pouring liquor into the gutter. In November, they coupled their anti-shebeen campaign with a call for a 'Christmas of mourning'.

To the migrants, these demands added insult to injury. If the residents couldn't drink in the shebeen, they argued, they (the residents) could always relax at home. But the migrants had no place other than the hostels to go to, because the students had already burned down the beer halls. The students had not respected them so why should they, the migrants, respect the students?

The students in their excitement did not discriminate between shebeens frequented by permanent residents and those whose clientele were largely contract workers. A gang raided a shebeen on December 2, in a Nyanga hostel run by and for members of the Baca clan, a group reputed throughout the townships to be among the most 'backward' and 'tribal' of all migrants in Cape Town. The hostel was gutted in the fight and two Baca were killed.

The migrants charged that the students were hypocrites. 'They threw out the Lieberstein,' Mr Luvado said, referring to a cheap wine, 'but when they came across the brandy, they put the bottles in their pockets.'[2] The following day, older residents of Nyanga met with the Baca, who accused them of having encouraged the students in the attack. The residents agreed to watch their children more closely, and after a Nyanga Residents' Committee had been established to improve relations, they made a tentative peace.

Yet the peace did not hold. The weeks that followed became a brutal commentary on apartheid and the policy of preventing new African settlement in town. To the government, the deepening hostility between the migrants and residents was a clear struggle between the 'good' African who understood that his place was in the country, and the 'bad' African who had become 'spoiled' and 'cheeky' as he had learned 'city tricks'. The migrants' reaction to the uprising confirmed to the ruling group the warning of Verwoerd and Eiselen that the African working class could only be controlled and prevented from colluding with coloureds if it remained migrant.

During December the police began to support and encourage the migrants' defiance of the students. Although no new strike calls were made, the police began to warn the hostel-dwellers that if the 'Christmas of mourning' campaign was successful, they would be fired and sent home. At the hostels of the Baca, a new shebeen had opened to replace one gutted by the students. When the men were drinking with their homeboys at midday, students raided again. They poured out the pots of beer, broke the bottles of wine and liquor, and attempted to set the room on fire.

Mr Luvado ordered other Baca to arm themselves after the students had retreated. 'I told them to put white doeks (cloths) on their heads, and white clothes on their bodies. We all had whistles and I, as a leader, had a bugle. When I blew it, that was the signal for everyone to come together. This is in accordance with our laws of battle where I come from.' About sixty or seventy men put on uniforms, collected knobkerries, axes, knives and other weapons and ran across Zwelitsha Drive, the road separating the hostels from the family houses. They captured and beat students in the area all afternoon.

During the next two days, the police and other government officials supervised the battle. Perhaps without being fully conscious of their prejudices, they revealed the old affection for the 'raw, untutored Kaffir' and their hatred of the urban African, whose 'city ways' were turning him to revolution. Mr Oscar Mpetha, who lived with his family off Zwelitsha Drive on Fourth Avenue, went outside with his son at 4.00 p.m. and found 'the contract boys' chasing students with sticks and stones. He broke up the fight momentarily and then approached a white policeman standing nearby. When Mr Mpetha asked him to help keep the migrants from crossing and beating the students, the policeman answered, 'They are your children.' When Mr Mpetha asked again, he was told a second time that 'They are your children.' Mr Mpetha then walked a mile to the police station to talk to the constable's superior. Again he was told that nothing would be done because 'they are your children.'

When sixty-eight-year-old Alfred Ndamase saw the fighting and went to the police station, he too was turned away with the words, 'They are your children.' And when Mr N Njokwana complained to a group of policemen sitting in vans that 'our children are being beaten up,' he had the same rehearsed reply.

Another constable told James Mlungaza, a resident of Nyanga, that he approved of what the Baca were doing. 'It is *those* people who were assaulted,' he said as he pointed to the hostels. 'You and your children are silly. You are black powers.' The policeman said that he respected the migrants and thought that they were stronger. 'Those people you talk about are the people who came from the country with us so we grew up playing sticks together in the reserves. You know nothing about sticks. All you know is about stone-throwing and bottle-throwing.'

The residents held a meeting about 7.00 p.m. to plan protection for the night. After a brief discussion, they lined up in front of their homes along Zwelitsha Drive armed with stones, clubs and knives. A group of migrants tried to storm the line between nine and ten o'clock that night. Two men who broke through ran behind a church which stood nearby. They were ambushed by a group of students. One was beaten to death while the other staggered away, his head bleeding.

The Baca crossed the road early the next morning to carry the corpse away. 'Some residents came over and told us to come and fetch our "dog" which they had killed,' said Mr Luvado. 'They told us we must all get on the next train back to the Transkei.'

Shortly after the body had been taken away, Mr Mpetha joined the residents guarding the houses, some of whom had been standing by the road throughout the night. He soon saw four police vans come down Zwelitsha Drive, and disappear up a road which led to the hostels. The migrants massed on their side of the road thirty minutes later. The four vans reappeared, crossed the street, and parked a few feet from the residents. One policeman jumped out of a van, raised his arm in the air, and beckoned to the migrants. The Baca charged across the street, and began to set on fire the houses which stood next to the church.

As the residents ran to protect their homes, the police started firing at them. 'They were in between us and the single men and they were shooting in our direction,' Mr Mpetha said. 'They were firing above us. We did not stand still. We ran.'

The residents finally succeeded in driving the attackers back across the street, but only after several houses were already gutted. Representatives of the two groups agreed to attend a meeting an hour later in the centre of Zwelitsha Drive 'for the creation of peace.' Mr George Ndesi, who attended the 'indaba', said that it had been called by the migrants. 'They said that the police had instigated the battle. But now peace had to be kept because blood had already been shed.'

It is unclear what happened next. Residents claimed that once the 'indaba' had broken up and they were heading back to their homes, the police began shooting at them again, and encouraged the migrants to continue the attacks. Members of the police and the hostel dwellers claimed that it was the students who had broken the truce. 'They killed three migrants and then poured petrol over their bodies and set them alight,' said Mr Luvado. 'By the time the police arrived, the residents had run away.' The migrants then prepared for more brutal retaliation. 'It was then that I decided that we should fix the residents because of what they had done to us,' Mr Luvado said. 'I blew my bugle and we attacked the residents, drove them back and set fire to their houses. I told my men to burn all the houses except for those with old people in them.'

The migrants and police worked closely together throughout

the day and deep into the night. Eye-witnesses gave the following accounts:

Angelina Makhaluza: I was standing in front of my mother's house. I looked out of the window and saw the bachelors enter through the front gate. She ran to the kitchen and looked through the window. From there I saw more migrants at the back yard and amongst them there were three policemen carrying 'baton sticks'. The migrants were breaking the windows of my father's car. The police did nothing.

I then ran into the back room. I heard a noise coming from the front of the house. I opened the door leading to the bedroom and saw the front door opened. One of the hinges had been broken. I ran through the kitchen into the yard outside where I saw my mother being beaten up by the bachelors outside the kitchen window. I got in between the bachelors who were attacking my mother. I spoke to the bachelors saying they should rather kill me instead of killing her. I was then dragged away and then someone said I must be killed and as a result I was chopped. My mother later died.

Mrs Deborah Luvuno: On Boxing Day I saw a crowd of migrants wearing white garments and white doeks on their heads coming down Sakkiesdorp Road towards Sixth Avenue. They were followed by three police vehicles. The migrants split into two groups and the police vans drove between them and out ahead of them. We saw a policeman sitting on the bonnet of the leading vehicle. He appeared to be beckoning to the migrants to follow. They had at first been coming very slowly and the policeman seemed to be making sure they were following. The police got out of the vans and crossed Sixth Avenue towards us. They were carrying guns. We heard gunshots and then we saw three policemen crossing the road towards us. I took the children inside the house and locked the door. I saw that the residents who had been standing along Sixth Avenue were running away towards Fifth Avenue.

From the front window, I saw the three policemen coming through the front gate. The last of them to enter made a sign to some migrants to follow him into the yard.

We moved away from the window and into the bedroom where we heard that the front door was being kicked in. There was a nasty burning smell and my daughter asked me to investigate. With the bedroom door slightly open I could see that migrants were burning the house.

I had once done laundry for one of the migrants. I asked him what I had done, and as I asked him this, another migrant came up to me with an axe in his hand. I went back into the bedroom and told my children the dining room was on fire. My older daughter went out the back door with two of the other children. 'I followed them, and when I was in the kitchen I saw there were some migrants at the back of the house. I went back to the bedroom, from where I heard screams — my daughter's screams — coming from the toilet. At this stage some of the migrants had come into the kitchen and I heard them talking about using something that would burn. One of them mentioned paraffin.

'One of the children broke the burglar proofing and jumped out of the window. I don't know how I escaped. I think I was helped by neighbours.'

The killing and burning continued into the early hours of the morning. Refugees lined the roads outside Nyanga carrying the few belongings they had managed to drag out of their homes. Many headed for Modderdam and other squatting camps. Within the next weeks, many permanent residents concluded that the legal and cultural distance between themselves and the migrants was too great to be bridged.

9. The Squatters Organize

THE COMMITTEE

Mr Simon Matthews had come to the camp shortly before the June 2 raid. When the shouting and fighting began, he stayed behind a bush out of the way. He had seen too many of these battles and felt too old to play these games. Yet during the next week, he visited every shack, organizing a committee to protect the squatters and keep order in the fast-growing camp. People were enthusiastic. Yes, they said, such a thing was important.

He called a meeting for the following Sunday, 'just to see who would show up.' About fifty people gathered in a clearing. Mr Matthews worried that it would be hard for such a group, who had only recently met, to decide anything. Yet surprisingly, they quickly formed a committee to see if water could be brought in and the police kept out. Ten men were chosen, with Mr Matthews the informal leader. 'It is time to come out of hiding,' Mr Matthews said. 'We have to tell the whites, "Here we are and this is what we have done. Now what are you going to do about us?" '

In their weather-beaten clothes, these 'bush bears' as the squatters sometimes called themselves, were an unlikely group of negotiators. Yet they worked well in those early months of the camp. They found an engineer to sink a borehole and test the water. Unfortunately, it was undrinkable. They discovered that the land on which they were squatting was owned partially by the Cape Divisional Council, the local government body, and partially by the Dutch Reformed Church. Their boldest action was to take their case to the local police stations. The men offered to maintain order inside the camp and to cooperate with the police on serious criminal offences if the officials did not enter Modderdam to arrest pass offenders. The committee was astonished when their offer was accepted. An informal agreement was made that as long as the camp was peaceful, there would be no more raids until the legal status of the camp was determined.

Word spread quickly throughout black Cape Town that a new shanty town was going up. Modderdam expanded in all directions. Shacks were erected daringly only feet from the road. To an observer looking solely at the land bounded by Belhar, Modderdam Road, the railroad track and the coloured parliament, it would have appeared as though the squatters had scared off the police during the raid and had won a major victory. The population of Modderdam grew from 400 to 10 000 between June and December of 1976. Yet it was not the squatters' resistance but that of the students which had stayed the hand of the police.

As the marching, stoning, demonstrating, burning and shooting swirled around the camp, Modderdam became an eye in the storm. Men still rose early for work and women slipped into Belhar for water. The Xhosa music blared as before. The only obvious response to the uprising was the sound of nails being hammered into metal sheets and wooden planks which could be heard all day and sometimes far into the night. Terrified by the violence, more and more migrants left the hostels for Modderdam. Women from up country who might otherwise have gone first to the hostels now went straight into the bush. Men who had long wanted to build their own shacks seized the rare opportunity of finding the police preoccupied. While it was the turmoil surrounding them which enabled them to build, the shanty town's survival depended on the squatters' ability to keep their community out of the fighting.

The committee met many times to discuss the revolt. The arguments were tense and sharply drawn, clearly reflecting the squatters' position: caught between the residents and the migrants. Those members who had come from the hostels or the homelands distrusted the students and felt strongly that the camp should be guarded to prevent them from using Modderdam as a hideout. Those more at home in Cape Town disagreed, saying that they themselves had taken the land without asking, and that they therefore did not have the right to refuse entrance to anyone.

Mr Plaatjie called for a compromise. 'The students can't help us,' he said, 'but it would not be good to be seen as their opponents.' He urged that members of the committee keep watch on the borders of the camp, but chase away only those directly involved in the fighting. Mr Matthews took a harder line. 'I was afraid that if we let in any of the "black power boys", they would try to take over the camp and the police would be here — whoosh — before you could turn around.'

Mr Plaatjie's suggestion was finally approved. Guards were appointed and placed on the road and the railway tracks and the residents were warned not to harbour students on the run. The regulation, however, was hard to enforce. One rainy night at the end of August, Mrs Phindi heard a knock on her door while she was cleaning her dinner dishes. She opened it and saw a young man, soaked, out of breath, with blood caked on one arm. He asked in Xhosa for food and a place for the night. She hesitated, then said, 'All right. The mpoqoshu is still warm. There is tea. You can stay if you leave before the sun.' She asked him not to tell her his name, address, or how he had come to be at Modderdam.

The people of the camp remained nervous bystanders of the uprising until the Nyanga battles. Then, as rumours spread that the refugees and the migrants were coming towards the camp, the squatters found themselves alone — as afraid of the hostel dwellers as they were of the students, and increasingly worried that the arrival of either group could trigger a police invasion. The committee again stationed people on the borders of the camp to screen and ward off new squatters.

WHITE HELP

The squatters' own fight started in earnest after the Christmas killings, when the student movement was collapsing. Yet despite the common root of the squatters' and students' fight these two resistance movements were not drawn closely together because of the distrust surrounding the 'civil war'. Had the government been so clumsy as to begin its campaign against the squatters at the height of the Cape Town rebellion, it is possible that the two groups would have worked closely together. Yet in the aftermath of the violence, the squatters had little choice but to distance their own struggle from that of the students. The fight for the shanty town was as political as the township uprising, yet the squatters initially presented themselves not as rebels but as humble people, who unlike the students, wanted simply to live quietly and do an honest day's work.

However this need and desire to cut themselves off from the turmoil around them also made it possible for the squatters to win white legal and financial assistance, and to appeal to white guilt and pity. Liberals no longer able to support black resistance as it turned violent could still rally around the squatters who were fighting for the simple right of African men and women to live in the city. The squatters' ignorance of political rhetoric and ideology thus made it possible for them to use white help at a time when the students had rejected any collaboration with whites.

Mr Matthews, who did much to establish the link between white churches and community groups, differed sharply from most of the other squatters both in his political awareness and in his understanding of the students' revolt. Yet he, too, believed in the importance of winning white friends and setting the squatters apart from the violence which surrounded them. His own political education in the 1940s and 50s had taken place at a time when whites worked closely with blacks in broader political movements. He had known several members of the old Congress of Democrats. When he was living in the squatter camp at Retreat, the group had even sent him to Johannesburg where he had met Mpanza, the leader of Shanty Town. He was convinced that white lawyers, journalists and ministers were needed to save the camp. Black students would only hasten the destruction.

In the early months of 1977, the people of Modderdam believed that the whites were their strongest allies. They were slowly disillusioned.

The wealthiest of the welfare organizations which pledged support was SHELTER, founded in February by an anonymous donor who sent R500 to the *Cape Times* after seeing an aerial photo of the camp on the paper's front page. Within one week, R51 000 poured into the office, and R300 000 had arrived after one month. Yet ironically, the organization proved to be of little help to the people of Modderdam, because the Trustees ruled that the money could only be spent for 'legal' squatter camps — those for coloureds or 'legal' Africans awaiting new homes. Dr Oscar Wollheim, a founder-trustee, stressed that SHELTER did not seek a confrontation with the government and could not use its money to improve the shacks at the camp. 'We do not think it sound economics to erect temporary structures which would be destroyed in a few months.'[1] Although Mr Wollheim and others personally abhorred the pass laws and the migrant labour system — and made several appeals to save the camp — they did not dare commit SHELTER funds, fearing that the organization would be disbanded. Six weeks after SHELTER was founded, Trustee David Hennessey stressed that 'in all our planning we have been very conscious to work within the framework of the law and to work with and through the local authorities. It could not be otherwise.'[2]

On this safe basis, SHELTER became the most popular charity in the city. The management and staff of Cape Auto Electric gave R60. The Green and Sea Point Hebrew Congregation gave R800,50. A group of schoolgirls organized a 40-mile bike-a-thon and raised R200. The Cape Town Round Tablers donated R100. Susan Shapiro, age 6, sent R5 in lieu of a birthday present. Artist Norah Cochran placed a contribution box at an exhibition held in her studio. 'Many generous people popped coins and notes in the box,' she wrote to the *Cape Times*, 'which in the end added up to R32. Just a drop in the ocean — but the drops add up too!'

Social work students at the Institute for Social Development of the University of the Western Cape came to help in the camp. Although they were coloured, they operated under much the same limitations as white community workers because the university was government-run and carefully watched. These men and women faced the dilemma of all social workers in South Africa. They could either focus on bringing health and educational services into the camp or on assisting the squatters politically. While the government tolerated soup kitchens, kindergartens and first-aid clinics, any 'agitation' was dangerous. The students assumed that one of their number or a supervisor was a Security Police informer, and knew that any political assistance must be given quietly. These dangers were made explicit during the first week of March when the Institute's director, Wolfgang Thomas, was deported.

The Cape Flats Committee for Interim Accommodation was the most overtly political organization working for the squatters. It helped finance legal fees, paid stipends to Mr Plaatjie and Mr Matthews to allow them to work in the camp full time, sponsored meetings and workshops for squatters from different camps, and provided liaison between the shanty towns and white liberals in

Parliament. CFCIA was funded by Episcopal and Catholic churches. While some within the organization believed it impossible to develop the resistance of the squatters and the sympathy of whites simultaneously, others felt the need to be sufficiently moderate to win financial support and prevent the organization from being banned. CFCIA workers lived at the margin of 'legitimate' protest. It was not unusual for a member to give a restrained speech at a Rotary luncheon or a Women's Club tea, only to be followed home by a member of the Security Branch.

SHELTER, ISD, and CFCIA worked loosely and imperfectly together. The frustration and tension of protest was such that as the fight became more dangerous, members within each group fought and distrusted each other. SHELTER was accused of selling out. ISD was labelled a government plant. Members of CFCIA were at times charged with trying to make martyrs of the squatters.

EARLY VICTORIES

In late January, the government announced its plan for the demolition of Modderdam. Coloureds and Africans would first be separated. Coloureds would then be sent behind Belhar to a new squatting site, Rifle Range. Africans would then be screened into 'illegals' and 'legals'. Rural women and children, as well as men who had neither contracts nor residence rights, would be given free railroad tickets to the Transkei and free baggage space for their belongings. Men with valid contracts would be sent back to the hostels. The few African men and women who *did* have full rights to stay in the city would be moved to a squatter camp on a plot of land called KTC near Nyanga. Squatters would be permitted one free truck load to transport both their possessions and their dismantled shacks.

The scheme, presented to the squatters' lawyer Richard Rosenthal by the Bantu Affairs Commissioner Fanie Botha, was a remarkable commentary on the consistency of apartheid ideology. It was, down to the smallest detail, the exact plan which Verwoerd had devised twenty years ago in dismantling Windermere and other shanty towns. While the structure of the economy had changed dramatically during those years, the government's understanding of African labour had not.

Under the Prevention of Illegal Squatting Amendment Act, passed the previous year, there was nothing to stop the demolition crews from levelling Modderdam as long as eviction notices were posted correctly one week in advance, and the squatters' property was not damaged. Mr Rosenthal told the squatters that an effective defence could be mounted only if the government broke its own laws.

Two eviction notices were posted on every shack by employees of the Department of Public Works on February 7. The first warned the squatters to leave within seven days. The second threatened 'dire consequences' if the first notice was not obeyed. As the notices were being tacked to the doors, one worker told the *Cape Times* that Modderdam was needed for the expansion of the University of the Western Cape, although 'not at the moment'. 'We must clear the land. We cannot allow permanent squatters.'

One day before the notices were to expire, the squatters were granted a two-day reprieve. Police vans arrived at the camp on February 11, but by the afternoon had worked out a second stay of execution — this time for seventeen days. Throughout the negotiations, the different legal groups of squatters stayed unified. Only one family accepted the government's offer to the 'legals' to move to KTC. Business was so bad at a mobile office which BAAB had brought to the camp to dispense railway tickets that the officials soon abandoned the idea.

On the Saturday afternoon before the end of the second reprieve, Mr Botha called Mr Rosenthal at his home and asked him to bring members of the squatters' committee with him to a meeting the following Wednesday. When Mr Matthews, Mr Plaatjie and the other squatter leaders were told of the proposal, they decided to hold a general meeting in order to receive instructions from the whole camp. The men took the invitation as an important sign that the committee was being given official recognition.

Six hundred people gathered that Sunday. The groups came out strongly against the plan to divide the coloureds and Africans. Several resolutions were proposed, stating that none of the squatters would move unless provisions were made for all within Cape Town. After more than two hours of discussion, the squatters authorized the committee to bargain with Mr Botha according to guidelines drawn up with the assistance of Mr Rosenthal. These instructions characterized well the modesty, firmness, and slight naiveté of the squatters' demands.

The committee described Modderdam as a 'close-knit, cohesive and law-abiding community,' which deeply wished to continue to live together as a community 'in view of the peaceful environment, the lack of crime and the community spirit that has been engendered.'[3] Although the people had been moved many times before, the committee said, they would move again, provided that alternative accommodation (with water, sanitation and garbage removal) was made available near public transportation. They would do this, however, only after receiving 'the categorical written assurance by the appropriate Minister that under no circumstances will they be required again to move from such a place, until adequate alternative housing is, in fact, available and offered to them.' But because these arrangements would take time, the squatters asked that Modderdam be declared an emergency camp for the interim. The squatters then appealed to the government with religious, not political or economic arguments. 'It is hoped that as an act of compassion, the State will recognise the right of families to live together with their menfolk who are lawfully at work in the city.'

The Wednesday meeting was the first of several between the squatter leaders and Mr Botha. It soon became apparent to Mr Matthews, Mr Plaatjie and the others on the executive committee that they had been brought there not to bargain, but to help the government disperse the squatters along apartheid lines. After Mr Botha had first taken down the names and legal qualifications of each of the executive committee members, the meeting broke up without resolution.

One day before the final expiry date Mr Matthews and Mr Plaatjie petitioned the Cape Town Supreme Court. The government had blundered, as Mr Rosenthal had hoped it might, by drawing up sloppy eviction notices. Senior Counsel L Dison, a partner in Mr Rosenthal's firm, argued in court that the notices were invalid because according to the new act, the order to dismantle a shanty had to be served directly on the person who had erected it. Mr Plaatjie's notice was made out to his wife, who was only an occupant. Mr Dison also claimed that the Public Works Department had no authority to knock down Mr Matthews' shack because the land on which it had been built had belonged to the Dutch Reformed Church — although the Church had subsequently turned the land over to the government. According to the same anti-squatting law, Dison argued, the shack could be dismantled without a court order only if it had been erected without the owner's consent. As the government had not owned the land at the time the shanty was put up, that consent could neither have been given nor withdrawn. Finally, the lawyer argued, the notices were invalid because they did not give the squatters the reasonable time, stipulated in the Bill, necessary to dismantle a camp the size of Modderdam.

The court, which had already lost most of its authority to halt the government, clung as tenaciously to these technical arguments as did the squatters' lawyers, for it was the only power it had left. Mr Justice Burger accepted Mr Plaatjie's claim that his eviction notice was incorrectly drawn, and ruled that while there was no indication that Mr Matthews had received the Church's permission to settle on the ground, nor was there any evidence that such permission had been denied. The squatters, he said, could suffer 'irreparable harm' if the shacks were dismantled before the legal situation was clarified. A stay of six weeks was granted.

Modderdam prospered under the court protection. Without the daily threat of a raid, the squatters enjoyed a temporary security which enabled the committees to run smoothly.

Mr Matthews and Mr Plaatjie were satisfied with their interim victory and found that they had new support and respect in the camp. Mr Matthews particularly relished discussion of the case, prefacing each of his observations with the disclaimer, 'Although I am not legally versed . . .'

He believed that the key issue the squatters would face next was whether or not an eviction was legal without alternative accommodation being offered to everyone. Asked whether he thought it possible that Marais Steyn could simply alter the laws if the squatters won in court, Mr Matthews laughed. 'Don't worry, some day we are going to put *him* in a pondokkie.' Mr Matthews also suggested that if they did have to leave Modderdam, the squatters should put their shacks up on the front lawn of the Minister's Cape Town home.

Mr Matthews and Mr Plaatjie returned to court on April 15 for the decision. Mr Matthews wore a faded grey pin-stripe jacket, a simple black tie, and black pants held up by red suspenders. Mr Plaatjie's pink shirt and dark green pants were too loud for the black furniture and rich-grained wood panelling of the hearing room. A few squatters who had come as spectators stood at the back. The judge, in a dark robe, was at the front, facing an array of lawyers representing different clients and cases. The two men sat for an hour, unable to follow the proceedings. Finally their names were announced on the roll. The government, the judge announced, had decided to drop the case.

Mr Matthews and Mr Plaatjie returned jubilantly to the camp. The word spread quickly throughout black Cape Town. That weekend, several new shacks were erected at the back of the camp. The new residents said they had come because they had heard that Modderdam was now safe. It appeared as though the strategy was working.

10. A New Law

The squatters' victory in court infuriated the Nationalist legislators because the anti-squatting bill had been passed the year before precisely to avoid such postponements. This time the government counter-attacked on the legislative front: it would make legal what had been found to be illegal.

Yet before the Nationalists rewrote the very law they had drafted, a bizarre drama took place which turned the plight of the squatters from tragedy to farce.

'FRONT-END LOADERS'

On February 9, the news that eviction notices had been posted at Modderdam quickly made its way to the House of Assembly. Lionel Murray, spokesman of the United Party, interrupted the proceedings and demanded an emergency debate to discuss the action.[1] Unless the government was stopped, he warned, bulldozers would soon be called into the camp.

'That is a lie,' shouted National Party member Cas Greyling.

'That is the most shocking thing I have heard in a long time,' added Minister of Community Development Marais Steyn. 'I must say with the greatest emphasis that in no circumstances whatsoever will any shack be bulldozed. On the contrary, I go further and say that if the government or any of its agencies should bulldoze any shacks we shall be guilty of a serious breach of the law governing the prevention of squatting . . .' Mr Murray's accusation was 'shocking', 'excruciating to contemplate'.

111

As the squatters began their negotiations with the Bantu Administration officials, nothing more was said in Parliament about the issue until the following week. Then, on the morning of February 18, the papers ran a front page picture of a shack being knocked down outside the town of Stellenbosch. As Mr Steyn entered the House, he was greeted with shouts of 'Bulldozer! Bulldozer!' while opposition members waved the newspapers in the air.

Mr Steyn was nonplussed. 'Bulldozer? What bulldozer? I haven't seen any bulldozers in pictures of the demolitions. Those were front-end loaders!' They were not used to knock down shacks, he said, but only to carry away walls, roofs and floors which had been pulled apart by hand.

Opposition members called bitterly for the minister's resignation. But Mr Steyn stood firm. 'You are not interested in my point of view,' he said the following day. 'You are just interested in making mischief, so you had just better go ahead and do that.' The pictures in the paper, he claimed, were 'obviously posed.'

Mr Steyn's defence became increasingly dubious as the week progressed. The Stellenbosch official who had supervised the demolition admitted that the 'front-end loader' had in fact been used to push over the shanty. 'It is our property and we are entitled to use whatever means we choose to break them (the shacks) down,' he said.

Yet despite the bravado, the squatters again won a slight victory, and Mr Steyn was publically humiliated. Two of the men whose homes had been knocked down brought suit and won. And as if to add insult to injury, the judge ordered the municipality to rebuild the shacks. 'The people are out in the open,' the judge protested. 'They were soaked and had a very wet weekend. I would expect a public body to make amends for this sort of thing.'

Early in March, a crew of demolition workers returned to the camp and rebuilt the shacks. When photographers came to take their pictures, they were chased away.

'COMMUNIST ELEMENTS'

Marais Steyn, stalled once again by a judge, tried a new tack two months later, which brought the anti-squatter campaign to its logical and frightening conclusion — the complete removal of all the legal rights of squatters. The Prevention of Illegal Squatting Act, 1977, was tabled on April 25. It is a remarkable document — calling in legal language for an end to all legal protection for squatters. The crux of the law is contained in section 1c:

> It shall not be competent for any person to ask for any order, judgement, or other relief in any civil proceedings of whatever nature in any court that are founded on the demolition or intended demolition or the prevention of the demolition under this section of any building or structure, or on the removal of any material or contents thereof from the land on which the building or structure was or is situated, and it shall not be competent for any court to grant or give such order, judgement or other relief, unless such person first satisfies that he has a title or right to the land on which the building or structure was or is situated, by virtue of which right he may lawfully occupy the land.[2]

The law also stated that a shanty could be knocked down and a squatter's belongings removed 'without any prior notice of whatever nature to any persons.'

In defending the Bill, Mr Steyn again laid the blame on the 'tear-jerking' liberals who had given him no choice. Referring to CFCIA, SHELTER, and the squatters' supporters in Parliament, he said that it was clear that there were forces at work 'whose object it is to encourage and perpetuate squatting in order to foment dissatisfaction and racial hatred and to discredit the Government and South Africa.'[3]

'How else,' he asked, 'does one explain the recent court cases which were aimed at thwarting the authorities when they wanted to take steps to put an end to illegal squatting, which constitutes a danger to society?'

'Money for court cases seems to be no problem for these indigent people, who have no right to be on the land in question and are breaking quite a number of laws, laws pertaining to entry, and to building and health regulations. Every possible technical point, however small, is seized upon to thwart any action against the scourge by means of protracted court proceedings.' These whites, he warned, were playing 'a dangerous game' by attempting to make 'heroes of law breakers and villains of authorities.'

113

Mr Steyn tortuously denied that the squatters' legal rights were in fact being abolished. They could, he said, still bring their claims to court as long as they 'can prove their title or rights to property.' If Africans owned land, of course, they would no longer be squatters.

The Minister then defended the clause which removed the need to post eviction notices. He complained that the 1976 amendment which required that an eviction notice be served on the builder of the shack was faulty, because it was very difficult to establish whether the people living in the structure had actually erected it. This loophole had to be closed, he said, but this did not mean that the squatters would not be warned before they were evicted. 'I want to give the assurance that the doing away of this statutory notice will not mean that there will be a less sympathetic approach to demolition than in the past.' It could, he said, be 'administratively arranged' that 'sympathy and understanding continue to be displayed in such cases.'

The impatience of Mr Steyn's opening remarks set the tone for the Nationalist side of the debate. Mr Albertyn further excoriated white liberals. 'The element which sympathizes with these people and which is trying to apply the brakes and to delay action as much as it can, is trying to idealize this so-called culture and have it take root and thereby be given ammunition to use against the government to symbolize it as an ogre.' While the actions of these whites seemed 'so naive and innocent, so full of compassion,' in fact, 'the sting is in the tail.'

'People with a poverty culture are the easy prey of political organizers, a prey without a sound judgement, and without insight, ready to be misled by the henchmen of anarchy and even revolution.'

Mr Albertyn's final defence of the amendment was a ringing invocation of the original Stallard doctrine that Africans were only in the cities to minister to whites. On what grounds *should* the squatters be entitled to legal rights in the city, he asked rhetorically. 'It was always the intention only to accommodate those we needed in white areas.'

Eric Louw, the third Nationalist speaker, expanded the attack on the white opposition into a conspiracy theory, arguing that squatters did not know how to build the camp themselves. 'How do they (the squatters) manage to set up their houses in rows, leave roads open and measure out communal areas? Do honourable members want to tell me that that does not show there was organization behind it, that there were people who planned this whole situation?' How else was it possible, he asked, that the population of Modderdam had grown to ten thousand in less than a year? 'Do we not have the right to assume that there is an organization which is settling those people there in an attempt to disrupt our orderly pattern of life?'

These organizers were, he said, not only in favour of increasing the black population in the Cape but also wanted integrated schools and black majority rule. 'We know too that they are the people who denigrate South Africa in the eyes of overseas countries. That is why they adopt this attitude; for no other reason and not because of the contents of an important Bill.'

Then, in a remark which foreshadowed the destruction of Modderdam, Mr Louw explained that eviction notices impeded the clearing of the shanty towns, because they made it impossible for the government to mount a surprise attack. It was possible, he said, that if shanty town residents knew when the bulldozers were to arrive they 'may try to impose their fictitious right of occupation of a certain property in a violent manner.' Furthermore, he asked facetiously, why should notices be posted? 'They did not give notice to the owner on whose property they have trespassed.'

The following day the debate deteriorated to slander. Mr S P Potgieter asked, 'Do honourable members know who the people are that are streaming in to this area? They are not honest people. The majority of them are rogues. They steal by day. They steal by night.' He said that they left their stolen goods a little way from their shanties, so that the police could not prove who stole them.

The white liberals were not 'tear-jerkers' but 'communist elements'. 'They are the ones who take delight in slum areas. These create a wonderful field of propaganda for them whenever it suits them; they act as agitators and inciters of the non-Whites. They incite the non-Whites to set fire to schools, churches and houses. Surely we all know who they are?'

To the opposition, long accustomed to being labelled as agitators, the progress of the squatter laws was representative of the entire policy of apartheid and the strategy of National Party rule. 'This whole approach of the ends justifying the means is diabolical and can lead to the worst kind of fascism, as we have seen in other parts of the world, in other periods of history,' said

Alex Boraine of the Progressive-Reform Party. Dr Van Zyl Slabbert hammered again at the economic argument he had spelled out the year before. Although 'a permanent open season on squatters' was being declared, all this would accomplish was a rotation of the shanty towns. 'The dwellings will be demolished in one area and the squatters will erect them somewhere else. Thus the Minister is whistling in the dark if he hopes that his kind of legislation will assist in solving the squatter problem.' It was the government, not the white opposition which was the real agitator. 'As sure as I stand here, there will be incidents as a result of the implementation of this legislation. There will be dissatisfaction. There will be frustration and anger.' In his rebuttal, Steyn argued that if the squatters had left quietly, the whole debate would have been unnecessary. But, he said, they had acted arrogantly. When the eviction notices were posted, some crumpled up the papers and threw them away. Africans tried to get around the law by 'intimating' that they were coloureds. Others pretended that they understood neither English nor Afrikaans. Municipal workers were threatened, and worst of all, the squatters had brought the government to court. 'I want to know how one can administer an Act if one makes certain concessions to people and is shown such ingratitude.'

These were, he said, 'the innocent and saintly squatter communities' whom the opposition had defended in their 'oh so solemn and pious speeches.' As people tried to hoot him down, Mr Steyn cried, 'I want to speak about the rights of the squatters, the wonderful rights of the squatters! Let us retain our perspective. These squatters are law breakers. They are trespassers and are encroaching upon the rights of others, persons whose rights are as sacred, if not more sacred, than theirs, because they are, after all, not breaking the law. Their occupation and enjoyment of that land is lawful.'

The measure was passed by 88 votes to 33.

GOING HOME

Shortly after the debate, I and my interpreter visited Modderdam to find out the reaction of the squatters to the new law. Of all the people we spoke to, we found only one man who was preparing to return home. We talked in the evening inside his shack, which was lit by a single candle. He was a young man with the high cheekbones characteristic of the Xhosa people. He spoke with intense concentration, as if trying to persuade himself as well as his listeners of the correctness of his decision. At the end of the discussion, in which he talked with little interruption, he asked us whether we could advise him to stay or leave. His eloquence and determination led us to believe that of all the people we had interviewed, he had the best chance of returning to, and maybe even prospering in the homelands. Three days after we had spoken with him, he sold his shack and left Modderdam.

'I am from the village of Udidi at Engcobo in the Transkei. I wanted to come to the cities to work for the cattle as my father did. I wished to go to Johannesburg, but at that time, they were only recruiting for the mines and I did not want to go for fear of going underground. My brother had once been injured there and my friends had told me stories of rocks falling and people dying. They had seen men's backs broken. And so I decided to come to the Western Cape.

'I first went to a farm in Malmesbury (north of Cape Town) on a contract. Although I received only R24 a month, that was not bad money because I did not have to pay for food as we were receiving monthly rations. Nor did I have to pay rent. After four years, I had bought two cows and four sheep. On the farm the Africans stayed in a compound. We milked the cows in shifts. I learned a lot on the farm. I learned the importance of self-reliance for the farmer who lived by working the soil. I used to watch as the wheat and corn fields were ploughed and cared for. I then began to realize that someday I would want to go back and try to make a living on my father's land.'

'How much land is there?'

'Quite a lot, although I do not know the exact amount. Yet we have never been able to make it work. I used to return there every year at December and renew my contract. But after four years, the work ran out on the farm and I found it hard to get another contract. It is a real problem when you lose your contract because you have to return to the country to get a new one, and then you wait up there until you are forced to come without one. You see, most of the contracts are filled now by the same people who leave the city to renew the contract.

'I decided to try my luck and just come down here again even though my pass was not right. I found a job as a garden boy, and

I was happy. But I was staying at the bachelors' quarters in Langa and the police would always be around inspecting passes. I decided that it would be best to leave the township and come over here in the bush. Things continued that way for several months. My employer never asked for my pass and I was making a few rands more than I had on the farm. I saved much less, though, because I had to pay for food and transport. But then I was arrested for my pass, and after the third time, I was sentenced to two months in prison.

'When I went in, I remembered what my father had always said about towns and how he told us that he had never been to prison even once, never had suffered as much as a scratch in the city and never assaulted a person nor was ever picked up. It hurt me that I was inside and it seemed as though I had become a criminal. I was in with thieves and other tough guys from the town. We would work every day on the prison farm, which was used to grow the food for the prisoners. We would be chased by the guards who called us 'Black Power' and said that they were teaching us Kaffirs a lesson.

'I began to think deeply about us Africans here and what I should do. I saw that there was little for us here in Cape Town. I realized that I had been able to save some money only because I had not yet married, and my family was still living mostly on the land. I saw how men here became too much taken up with city life. They spend their money here and take girlfriends, and their wives must come to join them because they receive nothing. And while in my village there are people who have enough land, when the wives are away many things are stolen, and sometimes the land itself is taken away by the chief because it is not being used. When this happens, the wives must stay in Cape Town.

'But I said to myself that for me, from the experiences I have been through, I do not want life here because as far as I could see, it is going to get worse for Africans. I knew I have to stay in the squatter camps. And I saw how at any time I could lose everything and just be told to leave. You can look at the new law and see that this is so.

'So I thought of these things over and over, and when my time was up, I went back to my employer. He said that he did not want to take me again until I had a proper pass. I cannot write, but I asked someone to write to my father about all that had happened. I said that I had the idea that I should rather go back to the kraal and sell most of the cattle so that I would have that little money to open a shop and use the money I made there for the farm. I would hope to hire a tractor and see if I can get some fortune for the soil.'

'And your father agreed?'

'Yes. He wrote back and said that since I was having these work troubles and arrests, I should return home to see what I can do. I waited for some weeks, but now, with the law, I have decided to leave.

'It will be difficult there, even though my mother is from the family of the chief. I am not relying on this to succeed. Rather I will depend on my wits and my being a man. That then is my plan. I am worried, though, that I may not be doing the right thing for I know I can leave, but I do not know if I will be able to come back. Perhaps I am lucky to be able to make this choice, because there are many others who cannot. But now I have made up my mind to make it a success at home. I have suffered enough here.'

11. The Camp Divides

The unity of the camp became strained in the weeks which
followed the passage of the new Bill. Mr Matthews and Mr Plaatjie
were accused of planning to abscond with camp funds and of
working too closely with whites. At the same time, men bickered
in the executive committee, and the judicial committee was
accused of levying unfair fines and of trying to enrich itself. Most
coloureds left the camp voluntarily during July and moved to the
legal camp on the other side of Belhar. This increased the
suspicion of many Africans that Mr Matthews and Mr Plaatjie
would leave when it was convenient. The 'village squabbles'
intensified as the plight of the camp became increasingly hopeless.
On the day before the bulldozer arrived, several squatters
threatened to burn down the two men's shacks, charging that they
had worked too closely with the whites. The bickering hampered
the squatters' ability to organize resistance inside and outside the
camp, enabling the government to move in during the week of the
first anniversary of the Cape Town rebellion.

AN OX FEAST

The standing of Mr Plaatjie and Mr Matthews in the camp was
closely tied to the court case. Squatters, particularly the newer
migrants, respected their command of English and their
sophistication in dealing with whites. The two men, who seldom
left the camp, showed their power and ability vividly throughout
February and March. After they had appealed successfully to the

court for a restraining order, they were even accepted as the leaders of the camp by members of the Public Works Department, who would often check with them while in the camp, in order to ensure their own safety. The squatters' respect for the two men was at its height during the week in which the government dropped the court case. This particularly impressed those who had been in less organized camps, had never worked with whites, and had not even known that there was any defence against the government other than stones and knobkerries. They took the news as a victory. At the following Sunday meeting, they voted to hold a feast in celebration and spend the remaining money from the legal fund to buy an ox to slaughter.

Mr Matthews and Mr Plaatjie, however, warned against such enthusiasm for they were aware that the new law was being proposed. They felt that such a feast was premature and might only delude the people. The R150 which some members of the executive committee wanted to use was being kept in the bank under the account of the Modderdam Squatters' Committee. There were three signatories — Mr Matthews, Mr Plaatjie and the lawyer, Mr Rosenthal. Both Mr Matthews and Mr Plaatjie refused to sign the money over to the committee. They wanted no part in a scheme which they believed would only squander funds which might be needed later on. When they began to speak out against the feast, a rumour spread that the two men only wanted to keep the money for themselves. It was pointed out that they were free to stay in Cape Town because they didn't carry passes. They worked so well with the lawyer that it would not be difficult for them to convince him to release the money to them.

It appears as if these suspicions were first voiced by Frank Tala, a member of the executive committee. How did it just happen, he began to ask, that the funds were under their names? Mr Tala was a nightwatchman at the BAAB offices in Langa. Many squatters saw him being dropped off at the camp by a police van in the early morning. He wore a long, shapeless, green coat with brass buttons which were embossed 'SAP' — South African Police. Some residents took his actions, manners, and clothes as clear evidence that he was an informer. Asking about him in the camp, I was told:

'He is a poison, a *real* poison.'

'He likes to get to people after it is dark. He buys you a bottle of brandy and then begins to talk into your ear.'

121

'He is a *bad* man.'

Yet although Mr Tala was not well liked, his charges were hard either to prove or deny. He had played on the African squatters' poverty, their distrust of coloureds, and their ambivalence towards whites. His attacks were like witchcraft accusations in which the *possibility* of guilt can be more powerful than any defence. It was never established whether the government had planted the rumours, whether Mr Tala had simply fanned doubts which had already existed, or whether he was attempting to increase his own stature in the camp. The effect, however, was to deepen the suspicions the longer Mr Matthews and Mr Plaatjie held out.

The in-fighting grew as the effect of the new Bill became known. Rather than vindicating the warnings of the two men, many squatters were angry at Mr Plaatjie and Mr Matthews for having led the camp to white help. Besides, wasn't it even more likely that the two men would disappear now that the court case was no longer valid? Mr Matthews and Mr Plaatjie did not want to give in to this pressure by simply handing the money over to the camp because they feared that that would be seen as an admission of guilt. In late May, however, they relented. They withdrew the money and handed it over to the committee. Mr Tala still argued that the funds should be spent on an ox. As the camp was going to be knocked down anyway, he argued, how else could the funds be shared?

The feast was held during the second week in June. The ox was slaughtered at the meeting place, and several of the squatters' supporters were invited. Both Mr Matthews and Mr Plaatjie boycotted the celebration. 'I would never so much as touch one piece of that meat,' Mr Matthews told me.

WHITE FEAR

The passage of the new Bill weakened the external as well as the internal opposition to the demolition of the camp. Because it drew the distinction between 'legal' and 'illegal' blacks more sharply than ever before, support for Modderdam became increasingly dangerous. By helping only 'legals' liberals in fact helped to segregate coloureds and Africans and so to perpetuate the migrant labour system. With all legal defences swept away, persons and groups sympathetic to Modderdam had to obey the law and plead for compassion or break the law and support violent or non-violent resistance.

SHELTER appealed to the government repeatedly to save the camp, yet stuck firmly to its decision to offer financial assistance only to those blacks with legal rights in the Cape Peninsula. The organization also announced plans to establish a 'core house' settlement for coloureds only. Squatters in this new camp would be moved into firmer zinc houses which could be extended easily at a later date. The SHELTER trustees thought it wiser to provide some new homes, rather than antagonize the government and be denied assistance.

The Institute for Social Development continued to supply basic health and food services in the camp. Shortly before the new Bill was announced, however, Brigadier van der Westhuizen approached the group and asked it to encourage the squatters to leave, and to help plan alternative accommodation. The request split the Institute. Some argued that their role as social workers was to provide for their clients' needs as well as possible, regardless of their personal beliefs. It was all well and good to protest, they said, but plans should be developed and the people should be warned, in order to lessen the hardship of the move as much as possible. Others said they refused to become the government's tool and claimed that the Institute would be shirking its responsibility if it ignored the squatters' political struggle. Although no formal decision was reached, ISD workers neither assisted the government nor actively shaped political resistance. Most felt they had little choice but to act like Red Cross volunteers — not responsible to either side of the growing confrontation.

CFCIA saw the caution of ISD as evidence that it was working hand-in-glove with the government, making it easier for the squatters to leave the camp. The charges levelled against students and supervisors were as difficult to prove or disprove as those against Mr Matthews and Mr Plaatjie. Because ISD volunteers were working in a government-supported institution, the accusations could never be convincingly rebutted. Members of CFCIA refused to meet with their ISD counterparts for fear that information would be reported to the Special Branch. CFCIA itself organized a public campaign within white churches to save the camp. Its actions were mild considering the nature of protest in South Africa. Neither it nor any other group, for example, attempted to smuggle guns or molotov cocktails into Modderdam — as students and cadres of the underground liberation movements had done in the townships during the Soweto rebellion.

The government's final campaign began in late June. Municipal workers knocked down St John's Church on June 25 with hammers and crowbars. When the committee made its protest, David Roux of the Bellville municipality answered, 'I cannot accept that it was a church. I think it was a dance hall and was used for squatter meetings.'[1]

Coloureds were served with pink eviction notices on July 1. Each shack-owner was instructed to dismantle his or her shack and take the material to Rifle Range, where they would receive a plot which they could rent for R8 a month. Five days later new notices were posted on African homes as well.

> You are hereby advised of my intention to demolish buildings or structures and to remove material from the land. Your attention is drawn to the fact that mechanical equipment will be used to demolish buildings or structures and that closed or locked buildings or structures will be summarily demolished and the material removed from the land.[2]

The notice then reiterated procedures for screening the camp which were identical to those Dr Verwoerd had outlined in 1954 — legal families to an emergency camp, illegal families to the rural areas, legal men and illegal women divided between the bachelors' quarters and the villages.

MR BOTHA PARRIES

Two days later, the squatters requested and received another interview with Chief Bantu Affairs Commissioner Botha, Brigadier van der Westhuizen and other BAAB officials. As in the previous meeting, Mr Botha asked each squatter to give his name, shack number, and legal status. The squatters then handed to the Commissioner a prepared statement similar to the one drawn up for the first meeting in February. Mr Botha's response to each point was recorded by Mr Rosenthal.[3]

'We wish to make it clear,' the squatters had written, 'that we want to live as families — husband, wife and children together.'

'I don't think anyone will fight you on that wish,' Mr Botha replied. 'But you can exercise that wish only in your homelands.'

'Where the father is absent,' the statement continued, 'children grow without parental guidance and discipline.'

'I agree. This applies to all races, all over the world.'

'We are aware that we come here as single men under the labour recruitment system and have no choice as to whether to bring our wives or not.'

'I differ from you a little. No one took you by the collar, and brought you here to work. It is your own free choice to come here. I know the arguments that there is no work in Transkei. But you have come here at your own request.'

'The separation of husband and wife promotes illegitimacy and divorce.'

'I agree.'

'We refuse to go to KTC (the emergency camp at Nyanga) because of negative experience there. (The camp had once been dismantled.) The legal-illegal categorization is not in our interest. We want to move to any land as a whole community — with legal guarantees against any form of persecution.'

'We are not proposing to move you to KTC. You must go back to where you came from. Only those who qualify and whose wives also qualify may go to KTC. Those people will be on a waiting list for houses.'

'We would also like to have some clarification regarding change of laws — especially the pass laws.'

'We fully realize that the influx control and pass laws give a great deal of hardship. The government is giving attention to these things, but as things stand today there is influx control and we must accept that. If this were not so, many more people would stream here. The government wants to see how influx control can be made easier. But so far as I am aware, they are not talking of abolishing it.'

'Laws should be changed to allow us to live as families — because we cannot continue living like this.'

'We can argue for a long time about this. But I can tell you this. That no law is going to be changed to allow all families from Transkei and Ciskei to come and live here.'

'We are concerned about mixed marriages in our community.'

'I am also concerned.'

'We have stayed as a peaceful community without violence and crime because we are determined to stay together.'

'I want to agree with you on this; it is commendable and it is a point in your favour. But you cannot stay here together.'

'We do not want to commit any violence. We are making an appeal to the authorities to help us out of our plight.'

'We have been trying for a long time to help you.'

'We are concerned about costs involved in our removal.'

'No one financed you to bring your wives here or to put up your shacks; nor are they going to finance you to put up new shacks.'

Mr Botha concluded the meeting by speaking to the squatters in general terms. 'We have a lot of sympathy for you,' he said, 'and with a lot of the things you are saying. But you have taken the law of the country into your own hands. You have nobody's permission to put up shacks and bring your wives here. That is like making your own laws. Since 1975 we have been advising people they should mend their ways and take their families back to where they came from. In 1975 there were cases that were won by squatters and as a result the law had to be changed. The law again had to be changed in 1977, which shows that the government must be serious in this thing.'

One of the squatters then protested that he had been born in the Cape and did not know the Transkei. 'But while I qualify under Section 10 to stay here, my wife is from Lady Frere and does not qualify. What must I do — divorce her?'

'You should have thought of the consequences before you married her,' Mr Botha responded.

'But love is love.'

Another squatter then asked whether a three-month extension would be possible. Mr Botha said no. 'I suggest that you start moving out from tomorrow; then you will not have to face the bulldozers. We'd like to get it done nicely.'

THE COLOUREDS LEAVE

Three thousand squatters and their supporters attended the weekly meeting the following Sunday. After listening to men and women talk of their lives in the homelands and in the Cape Town bush, the crowd unanimously resolved to resist the government passively by simply refusing to move. In the passion of the meeting, they also agreed to undertake a three-day fast, and invited those outside the camp to join them. Mr P J Nelani told the press, 'We want to appeal to all churches . . . to join us as a mark of solidarity with us in our stand against the separation of families.'[4] The head of the predominantly white Women's Movement endorsed the fast and also urged members of her organization to sleep alone at night, to symbolize the separation of husbands and wives.

One coloured woman stood up during the meeting and expressed coloured solidarity with the Africans. Yet this was largely broken the following week when most coloureds obeyed their eviction notices, dismantled their shacks, loaded the material onto Divisional Council trucks, and left for Rifle Range. The Plaatjies and Mr Matthews had torn up the pink notices which authorized them to move to the new camp, yet they could get few others to follow suit. Several of the men and women said that Modderdam was going to be knocked down anyway and thus they had little choice but to accept the best deal offered to them. There were, surprisingly, no fights between the Africans and coloureds during the weekend. Some of the Africans, in fact, thought that it was just as well that they had left. Now the resistance was down to a hard core which had little choice but to fight, they argued.

Although the mood in the camp became more aggressive as the coloureds left, the committee tried to mediate with the government once again, by going over Commissioner Botha's head. They drafted a letter to the Deputy Minister of Bantu Affairs, Wilhelm Cruywagen, proposing a meeting and the creation of a 'liaison committee' to work between BAAB and the squatters. The letter, however, never reached Mr Cruywagen. Mr Botha replied that he was 'not in a position to recommend that Mr Cruywagen make himself available to the squatters.'[5] And while he had no objection to the squatters designating representatives 'out of their Bantu ranks', they would only be allowed to work with BAAB if they assisted in sending 'legals' to KTC and 'illegals' back to the homelands.

Two weeks before the demolition, Mr Botha forwarded a letter to *Die Burger* which he said he had received from an unnamed 'scholar'. Some observers thought that the scholar was Mr Botha himself.[6] The argument presented a view of African society unchanged from Verwoerd's idealized migrant who longed for his village. It attempted to justify the division of husbands and wives as a custom rooted in Xhosa culture. 'The plea of black squatters in the Western Cape that they wish to live with their wives and children was not their own,' the letter stated. It had been 'put into their mouths' by white philanthropists. The African was 'spiritually and socially completely different' from the white. 'As a nomad, as a stock farmer, and as a reaper he necessarily spends long periods away from home.' Furthermore, because it was traditional in black society for a man not to have intercourse with his wife while she was 'suckling', it was logical for him 'to satisfy his needs elsewhere.' Thus, the letter concluded, migrant labour was a 'good and acceptable substitute for the lifestyle of previous generations.'

Rev David Russell, the Anglican priest whose parish included the squatter camp Crossroads, addressed a student protest meeting at the University of Cape Town the next day. He told several stories of women being torn from their husbands and children, and ridiculed the letter in *Die Burger*.

TABLE VIEW

Shortly before the students filed out of the auditorium, one of the organizers of the protest announced, 'Now, as you sit here, a camp is being destroyed.' Forty shacks had been knocked down in driving rain near a white housing development called Table View. As some of the squatters had been living there for as long as three years, it appeared as though the shacks had been selected as a warning to Modderdam. When BAAB was criticized the following day for conducting the raid in the rain, Brigadier van der Westhuizen protested that 'people who were pleading the case of the squatters seemed to overlook that people also arrived in the Peninsula in the winter.[7]

'Bantu have been coming into the Peninsula area at the rate of 2 000 a month, and while one hears objections to these people being asked to move out in winter, one does not hear objections to the fact that they are streaming into the Peninsula at an escalating rate — in the winter as well as in the summer months. Where there were 25 000 Bantu squatters in the Peninsula at the end of June last year, there are now 51 000, and this is creating an intolerable situation with health and unemployment.'

There was a fight at Modderdam on Sunday, August 7, at the weekly meeting. It began as a debate over the strategy used to try to save the camp. Several men complained that collaboration with sympathetic whites had been a mistake. They said that while at first it had been good, now they were exactly where they had been in the beginning — before the law suit, the newspaper articles, the SHELTER fund, the social workers, and everything else. They said that they should have fought alone. 'What do we need those white people for?' they asked. 'We are people from the bush.' The men wanted to know why Mr Plaatjie and Mr Matthews had worked so closely with the lawyers and community workers. Did the two expect to receive anything from the whites in return, they asked. The two men were not sure whether the others were simply posturing. Mr Matthews argued back loudly that if it hadn't been for their work, the camp would have been gone long ago. 'Burn down my shack. I don't care,' he taunted. He didn't care. The argument gradually cooled. No one was hurt and nothing was destroyed. Yet plans for resisting the bulldozer were ignored in the quarrel.

PART 4
The Demolition

12. The Bulldozer Stalls

For as long as Africans have lived in the city, they have faced whites who have demanded that they remain migrants and villagers. Each confrontation has become increasingly desperate. The government has succeeded in knocking down homes and arresting 'illegals' but invariably they have refused to abandon the city — thus setting the stage for the next, bigger battle.

During the week of August 8, this classic South African drama was played out at Modderdam. At first, no one knew what to expect.

THE FIRST SHACKS

Mr Matthews awoke early Monday morning, August 8, with a headache and back pains. He washed his face in the white metal basin left out the night before. He dressed in brown pants, grey shirt and red suspenders, put on his hat and walked towards Mr Plaatjie's house. He wanted to discuss yesterday's fight.

As he walked down the path towards the road, his friend called to him. Mr Matthews looked up and saw Mr Plaatjie standing with his wife on the mound behind their house, pointing towards the right hand corner of the camp. 'They've come,' he shouted in Xhosa. Mr Plaatjie helped Mr Matthews up the hard-packed sand. From the top, he could see several police vans and white Volkswagens parked on the far side of Modderdam Road. A crowd of policemen were waiting to move into the camp. Rush hour traffic was stopped so that a yellow 'front-end loader' could be driven across the two-lane highway to the shanties. African men in dark brown overalls and orange helmets were standing on the pavement next to the camp, holding crowbars and shovels. Mr Matthews could hear a man with an electronic megaphone announcing in Afrikaans and Xhosa that the demolition would begin within fifteen minutes.

Men and women were running in and out of their houses, frantically dragging out wardrobes, beds, tables, chairs, suitcases, pots, blankets, clothes, dishes, and food, and carrying them towards the road. Women whose husbands had already left for work were dashing to other sections of the camp looking for help. Mr Matthews and the Plaatjies ran down the hill and across the camp to a shanty which stood only thirty feet from the pavement. A woman, her baby strapped on her back in a blanket, was throwing her possessions out of the door. Two men were struggling with a wooden-frame bed. Mr Plaatjie and Mr Matthews grabbed a straw mattress which lay on the floor, and slid it outside while Mrs Plaatjie gathered everything she could find into a pile and carried the utensils and clothes to the road.

The shanty was cleaned out just as the bulldozer drove down the short mud incline. The shovel of the Michigan Big Cat dug under the wall nearest the railroad tracks and lifted the corrugated iron fifteen feet in the air. The machine reversed to the right, and dumped the sheets. Then the driver brought the shovel around to the far wall and scooped again. With the rest of the shanty in its mouth, the truck drove forward, knocking down the last two wooden poles and twisting and crushing the debris in its path. As the bulldozer moved to the next shack, a white man ordered the African clean-up crew into the camp. The men began to break apart the fallen walls, stacking the zincs in piles and loading them into a large truck.

As Mrs Plaatjie helped others evacuate their homes, the two men left for the University of the Western Cape. The staff of ISD had already notified the press and other welfare organizations. Mr Matthews called Mr Rosenthal to ask him to arrange one final meeting with the Bantu Affairs Administration Board. Edna van Harte, a coloured lecturer at the Institute, asked the two men whether they thought emergency relief should be brought into the camp. The men responded that it was too early to know exactly what was happening. It was not yet clear whether this was the beginning of the demolition of the entire camp or whether it was just another form of harassment. But by the time the two men returned to Modderdam, another ten homes had been knocked down and furniture lined the pavement along the entire length of the camp. Residents and passers-by had gathered along the road. Policemen paced in groups along the curb, holding Alsatians at short rein. Mr Plaatjie and Mr Matthews walked back into the camp to help clear more homes.

I received a call from a student at ISD at about 10.30 a.m. 'They've started.' I collected my passport and car keys and set out along De Waal Drive past Groote Schuur — Cecil Rhodes's old estate. I drove through the once-integrated, working-class neighbourhoods of Observatory and Mowbray, then into the Cape Flats. There was no roadblock on Modderdam Road. I parked my car at Belhar and walked up the railway bridge to get a view of the whole shanty town. The bulldozer was stuck in the mud. Hundreds of blacks and whites were lined along the road. Police were making only feeble attempts to break up the crowds. The land nearest the pavement looked like a refugee camp, with furniture and clothes strewn together. Women with babies on their backs and at their breasts stooped on top of their possessions. A few were attempting to boil water on their primus stoves.

I walked towards the camp. Two groups of squatters were gathered in circles several yards from each other. At the centre of one, a light-skinned woman with a black shawl and a floral apron was holding her hands high in the air, addressing the crowd. They began to chant the hymn 'Jerusalem' in Xhosa. Four policemen with dogs were standing a few feet away, ordering the people to disperse. They began to move away gradually, but one woman stood still. Without warning, one of the dogs flashed towards her. She screamed and ran to the rest of the group who helped her onto the sidewalk. Her right leg bled heavily. The other people were gathered around two ministers of the Zion Apostolic Church. The taller man was dressed in a long green robe and a white cloth hat. He walked, then ran, around and around in a small circle dancing and shouting ecstatically. The shorter man, in a bright red robe, followed him beating a drum with a wooden mallet. The crowd began to sigh, shout, and dance. The taller man stopped abruptly after ten minutes, raised his hands and prayed loudly. He then lowered his head and the

132

crowd was quiet. The service was over and people slowly began to walk away.

The residents who stood apart from these gatherings appeared more sullen than aggressive. Some who lived in shacks far from the bulldozer were stubbornly carrying out their daily routine — washing clothes, cooking, and walking with plastic jugs to fetch water from Belhar. I found Mr Matthews near the road, walking towards a station wagon which was being used to take the woman bitten by the dog to the hospital. 'Oh, Hello there!' he said in his precise and gentlemanly manner. He then shook his head back and forth several times and walked away. I heard a woman call, 'Hey, Mr Andy!' Mrs Phindi, the businesswoman I had interviewed and usually greeted in the camp was sitting on a mattress knitting. Piled next to her were stocks from her store — small packets of sugar, coffee, tins of jelly, and oranges. She said that her house had not yet been hit. She did not think that it would be destroyed for a while because it was in the middle of the camp. She hoped to sell out her stock that day. I asked her if she had decided whether to leave or where she would go next. She laughed. Mr Plaatjie was standing next to his house. He said he had not begun to pack up his house. With the bulldozer stuck, he thought that there was little danger for that day. He also thought that the whole operation might be a ruse to scare the squatters into taking down their own shacks. At any rate, there was too much else to be done. He was most worried about sick or pregnant women who faced the night in the open. In the chaos of the following week, I tried to keep track of Mr Matthews, Mrs Phindi, and Mr Plaatjie. I also spoke with them after the camp was destroyed to find out more closely what they had seen, thought, and done during the demolition.

FINAL APPEALS

The government had planned its operation well and caught the residents and their supporters off guard, yet it had made little provision for transportation, food or medical care as the houses came down. BAAB officials had parked a van near the railroad bridge where 'illegals' could receive free tickets to the Transkei or Ciskei. Permits were also being distributed to 'legals' who wanted to erect shacks at KTC. Yet during the day, fewer than a dozen squatters asked for tickets or permits. Several hundred residents would be left all night with no shelter or emergency aid.

The bulldozer remained stalled for the entire afternoon. A tractor tried to haul it from the mud about 2.30 p.m. but it, too, became stuck. The squatters cheered and laughed. This delay gave the residents and community workers time to organize. Shortly after I had spoken with Mr Plaatjie, he met with Mrs van Harte for the second time. She had come to the camp to offer the assistance of ISD. They decided that food, medical care and some basic shelter were needed urgently. It was hard to find members of the committee, but Mr Matthews and two others agreed. Mrs van Harte returned to UWC and spoke with the University's principal, Dr Richard van der Ross. He was anxious for students connected to the Institute to work in the camp, in part to prevent the demolition from provoking boycotts and demonstrations on campus. He saw no way in which the students' anger could be contained unless members of the University were directly helping the squatters. Dr van der Ross drove out to Modderdam in his Mercedes Benz and met with Brigadier van der Westhuizen, the man directly supervising the operation. The Brigadier reluctantly agreed to allow ISD to set up a 'crisis intervention' station. He warned, however, that if the students were found 'agitating' the camp would be entirely sealed off.

The needs of ten thousand people had to be met by night-fall. Bread, milk, soup, vegetables, cardboard boxes, plastic tarps, cars, blankets, tents, first-aid kits, doctors and volunteers had to be found. One worker was stationed at the ISD office where she phoned private companies, churches, charities, and service groups. SHELTER refused to provide any aid not specifically approved by BAAB. One trustee drove out to Modderdam and pleaded with Brigadier van der Westhuizen to allow plastic tarps to be brought into the camp in order to protect the squatters' possessions from rain. At first he refused, arguing that the squatters would simply use the tarps to build new shelters. Yet he relented later in the afternoon, and huge rolls of plastic were delivered from a local camping equipment factory.

Mr Plaatjie helped students survey the camp and assemble a sick list. He began at a shack which stood directly in the bulldozer's path and gradually worked towards the back of the camp. He first found an old man wrapped in a blanket on his bed who said he was too ill to get up. A little further away, a woman was hiding in

134

her house with two sick children. She said she was afraid to leave because of the police in the camp. She feared she would be arrested and taken away from her children.

The Plaatjie's house and a green four-man tent erected next to it became the headquarters for the relief services. The living room was first used as an office for the University of Cape Town medical students who arrived in the middle of the afternoon. The kitchen was the waiting room. Mrs Plaatjie was stationed there, preparing tea for the volunteers and the patients. After an hour, Mr Plaatjie had assembled a list of twenty people. He returned to his house and brought a doctor to attend the sick. The people were then taken in private cars to Tygerberg Hospital, ten minutes away.

Food brought into the camp was initially stored in the tent. Twelve thirty-gallon aluminium containers of steamy vegetable soup were donated by the Pick 'n Pay supermarket chain and placed between the tent and the shanty. Women and children lined up with their bowls to be served. One woman student ladled the soup while another handed out fresh bread. Many squatters were convinced the food came from the government. They refused to look up at the people filling their bowls, and did not thank them as they walked back to their belongings. In the frenzy of the demolition, neither the volunteers nor Mr Plaatjie had time to question whether the relief enabled the squatters to stay longer at Modderdam, strengthening their resistance, or whether it only reduced a tough, self-sufficient community to dependence on charity.

Mr Matthews and other committee members received word during the afternoon that Mr Rosenthal had set up the meeting with Bantu Affairs Commissioner Botha. A student from ISD drove them to the meeting at the BAAB offices in Goodwood, a few miles away. Sunday's fight was forgotten in the crisis. The meeting with Mr Botha was as fruitless as the previous ones. This time the squatters did not bother to ask for alternative accommodation, but begged for a week's grace during which time they would ask the residents to dismantle their own shanties. The committee also asked that ISD, CFCIA, and SHELTER be permitted to erect tents near Modderdam for those who would be without a roof that evening. Finally, they urged Mr Botha to restrain the police and their dogs.

The Commissioner denied all three requests. The committee's

repeated refusal to respect the evacuation deadlines gave him no reason to trust their word, he said. He complained with exasperation, 'I have never known people to be so obstinate. There is no bargaining on this. When the government speaks, you must listen.'

The committee then asked Mr Botha what would happen when women returned to the homelands with no money, food or land. 'Where are we to go and what are we to do? We have wives and children who depend on us.' The Commissioner replied as he had previously that no one had invited them to Cape Town in the first place. Furthermore, he said, the stories of malnutrition and unemployment in the rural areas were largely propaganda. 'As a responsible government official, I can assure you that this thing of people starving in the homelands is overrated.' Mr Botha then turned to the squatters and asked for their sympathy. He understood that it was difficult for them, but *they* had to understand that it was difficult for him as well. 'This is one of the most unpleasant things I have had to do in all my forty years of government service,' he said. When the half-hour meeting was over, the committee issued its final statement. After reporting Mr Botha's response to its proposal, it said defiantly, 'If we are criminals, then our crime was to live with our families.'

Mr Matthews returned to the camp convinced that there was no possibility now that the demolition would be postponed. He was forced to consider questions he had put off for several months. 'When should the camp be abandoned? How long should the squatters attempt to occupy the land with no shelter?' Reporters had asked him these questions several times and he had replied with bravado, 'We will let them knock our homes down. We are non-violent. How can we stop them? But we will then tell them, "Fine, now what are you going to do with us?" ' Mr Matthews realized, however, that the internal organization of the camp was no longer strong enough to support such passive resistance. Even if it was, the cost might be too high. He knew that sooner or later the squatters would have to leave and if they left now, the greater their opportunity would be to find a new place. It would be cruel to encourage people to stay outside in the wind and rain of the Cape winter just for a few more days of defiance. As he talked with other squatters, however, he was surprised to discover that few had made plans to leave. He heard three rumours. The bulldozer was only being used to frighten the squatters. White students and clergymen would halt the demolition the next day. The government's rail tickets were good only up to De Aar or Worcester, a few hours away, and after that the squatters would have to pay the full fare home.

WAITING

Mrs Phindi sat in her makeshift stall the whole afternoon watching the police and crowds. When she was not making a sale, she knitted a green cap. She was planning to sell it and three others she had made the week before for R1.50 at her brother Simon's hostel in Guguletu, Zone B.

Simon lived with his room-mate John in one of the long brick buildings which were sub-divided into two-man rooms. Mrs Phindi had often sold clothes there and had even lived in the hostel for a time before coming to Modderdam. When she had left last December, Simon had told her, 'This is your room.' He had made her promise that she would come back if she was homeless again. She had been thinking about returning, yet she had been told the same story three times that day already: it is useless to hide in the hostels, people said, because the inspectors will be in and out of the rooms looking for you every night. Mrs Phindi also thought briefly of leaving Modderdam for Steenberg, where she had stayed a few years earlier. She still had many friends there willing to take her in for a time. Yet she was afraid that the raids at Steenberg might be as severe as those in the hostels. She decided that it was too early to move. She would wait to see where others would go.

Business was good. People were hungry and there was little competition from other sellers. The wealthier merchants had already fled Modderdam, loading up their trucks and driving away quietly. Most of the other traders were too excited or disorganized to bring out their goods. By late afternoon, only a few bags of coffee were left and four new rands in change were in her purse.

I stood on the pavement until mid-afternoon with groups of white and coloured students. The coloureds were particularly disgusted with the presence of the African workers who spent the day piling up the remains of the crushed shacks. It was, they said, the final indignity that these men were probably contract workers as well. 'You are the *real* kaffirs,' one student said as he pointed to them. His friend told him he was attacking the wrong target. 'What can they do? If they don't do their jobs, they *too* will be sent back to the Transkei.' The police appeared more concerned with the white spectators than with the squatters because they feared the whites would use their privilege to protest more provocatively. Several whites who tried to walk into the camp to help collect furniture were quickly chased back to the pavement. One middle-aged man kept dodging in and out of the camp until he was threatened with arrest if he did not leave Modderdam. He began to cry.

I left the camp about 3.00 p.m. and drove to the University of Cape Town to see if any demonstrations were in progress. I parked in front of the steps leading to Jameson Hall, long the centre for student protests. All was quiet. People were sitting on the steps leading to the building, sunning themselves and eating. Many were reading the *Argus* which carried the news of the demolition and an interview with Brigadier van der Westhuizen. 'So far the squatters have not moved,' he told the reporter, 'and those who want to have been intimidated so that, out of fear, they have been unable to negotiate with the authorities. In the meantime, large numbers of people are streaming for the Peninsula. The unemployment and health hazard is increasing. These people who are streaming in and disregarding all laws will eventually suffer most. The situation cannot be allowed to develop any further and everything possible must be done now to stop it.' Asked whether he thought the squatters would continue to resist, he responded, 'It is my opinion that they actually want to move.'

All non-class gatherings had been banned on the UCT campus by the local magistrate. Those who were interested in protesting were told to go out to the camp itself.

When I returned late that afternoon Modderdam had become a large traffic jam. Policemen frenetically tried to prevent returning workers from stopping on the road. A second tractor had entered the camp and was using a winch to haul out both the first tractor and the bulldozer. After fifteen minutes of pulling and rocking, the two vehicles were free. The crowd booed. Drivers climbed into the cabs, drove them up onto the pavement and out of the camp. The crowd cheered. As the convoy disappeared over the railway bridge, the officials began to move towards their trucks and vans, and spectators walked away. Many whites who had been there the whole afternoon decided to leave for fear that as their contingent dwindled, it would be easy for the Security Police to see them. Yet the whites who moved into the camp were only assisting in the most basic relief work — packing boxes, covering furniture, serving food.

I walked to the tent and found Mrs van Harte. She asked if I would drive out to the suburb of Wynberg and pick up vegetables from a coloured wholesaler who collected damaged produce from supermarkets and distributed it to orphanages and charities. I left with a student who had worked in the camp since February. As we loaded up my Volkswagen with potatoes, lettuce, beats, carrots, turnips, and apples, he laughed: 'I wanted to be a Che Guevara, but instead I have become a Florence Nightingale.' We stored the food in a walk-in refrigerator in the new cafeteria of the women's dormitory of the UWC campus and then helped load containers of hot powdered milk onto a truck bound for Modderdam.

In the dark, the camp looked like a place for hikers, not squatters. Men and women were keeping warm around small fires while they ate, talked, sang, and smoked. The tent had been replaced by a Winnebago camper donated by a wealthy coloured businessman. Inside the cabin, water was boiling on the gas range, a curry was cooking, and two social work students were slicing bread for the crowd still gathered outside. A camp meeting had finished half an hour earlier. Several of the squatter leaders had spoken bravely, vowing to remain even without shelter and urging all to stay together. Many of those who heard the speeches thought them to be only sad rhetoric. People cried at the end when the crowd held hands and sang the African National Anthem, Nkosi Sikelel' iAfrika — God Bless Africa.

I found Mr Plaatjie and Mr Matthews in Mr Plaatjie's living room. They said they felt partially responsible for the camp, yet realized that the committee had lost almost all power and control. Tomorrow would be crucial, they said. Had they decided where to go? Mr Plaatjie said he would stay as long as possible and then return for a while to his wife's parents' place in Factreton. Mr Matthews said he had a few ideas, but didn't want to discuss them yet. Both angrily refused to go to Rifle Range.

Mrs Phindi was tired. After the bulldozer had left, she returned to her shack and packed it up. She decided to move out everything the following morning. She complained to me that the whites who were trying to help had made a big mistake. 'They should have tried to get us another piece of land, instead of telling us that we should try to keep this one.' The wind was strong and the air felt as though it might rain. As I walked towards the road, I saw that a new shanty town was being built. Brigadier van der Westhuizen had been right. Squatters whose homes had been knocked down in the morning were using the SHELTER tarps as walls and roofs for new shacks. The structures were just big enough to sleep two people.

The coloured social workers spent the night in the caravan. They were woken at one and three in the morning. Policemen were checking to see if any whites were still in the camp.

13. Modderdam Burns

During their long campaign, the squatters had moved quickly through the stages which mark the evolution of revolts throughout the world — from legal appeal to public protest to civil disobedience. On Tuesday, August 9, the resistance moved inexorably towards violence.

The appeals of the white sympathizers had failed and the government had begun to smell victory. On the front page of the *Cape Times* a letter from the man whose R500 donation had sparked the SHELTER fund six months earlier, was framed by a black border:[1]

> I cannot yet believe my own eyes, but today I saw through them the most heartless, most conscienceless treatment of human beings that some of my fellow-countrymen have meted out to the have-nots on Modderdam Road. The misery of the ejected squatters with their homes in ruins, guarding their meagre possessions on the roadside is indescribable. If ever we were entitled to describe our country as Christian, that description has today lost all the meaning it ever held for me. As a so-called white South African, I have to share the guilt of the 'haves' of contemporary society. I hang my head in shame and plead for forgiveness. When one day we are called to account in God's judgement halls, what will be our defence when the Judge, the King himself, declares, 'Inasmuch as you have done it unto the least of these my brethren, ye have done it to me.'

The second article, on the following page, carried the text of a circular from the Cape Divisional Council, distributed a few days before the demolition had begun:

> As you probably know, the provisions of the Prevention of Illegal Squatting Act of 1951 have already been made applicable to the whole of the Republic and in the interest of everybody concerned, you are once again called upon to render your esteemed co-operation in effectively combatting the squatting evil — especially now that the Amendment Act has removed previous encumbrances like the compulsory serving of a notice and a ready access to the courts on trivial grounds.[2]

SKIRMISHES

The following morning it was cold and overcast. Winds off the Indian Ocean created small clouds of sand. The mood of the camp had changed with the weather. The restraint of the police had given way to a determination to finish the job. The squatters' shock had turned to anger. The bulldozer was flanked by policemen on all sides. Each shack was first surveyed by four officials carrying walkie-talkies. They marked out the best line of approach and made sure the structure was vacant and free of booby-traps. There were rumours that deep holes had been dug underneath some shanties. Instructions were then given through the walkie-talkies to the driver in the glass-enclosed cab. The machine moved fast and efficiently, zig-zagging eastward across the camp.

The strategy of the police was to separate the squatters from their supporters and then break up all crowds on both sides of their human barricade. Only squatters, volunteers and reporters were allowed into the camp. As the tension increased throughout the day, the relations between the police and the volunteers improved as the officials realized how indispensable the medics and social workers were in forestalling a full riot. Confrontations between squatters and police shifted as unexpectedly as the winds. Most clashes were small — a few stones, a quick baton charge, a nervous face-off in which neither police nor squatters budged.

Mr Matthews cleaned out his shack early in the morning and

passed the furniture along a human chain which stretched from the road deep into the camp. One person would pick up a chair, walk it a few steps and hand it on. Mr Matthews was surprised at how smoothly the group worked together, for the continual advance of the bulldozer had begun to create panic elsewhere. Here the people's anger was tempered by the scramble for furniture. Mr Matthews believed that if the squatters had emptied their shacks the night before, a riot would have started early that morning. He tired of working on the chain after a few hours and decided to leave the camp for a while. The committee seemed to have disbanded and he didn't see what further use there was for him. He wanted to rent a truck from a friend at Unibel and see if he could find a shack there. As he walked up the railroad tracks, the sounds of the camp faded and he realized that he was glad to get out. He expected more violence.

Mr and Mrs Plaatjie again decided not to empty their house. The doctors had moved to the caravan, yet the Plaatjies still believed that their shanty was not in immediate danger. Mrs Plaatjie, in fact, decided to clean up the place because visitors would be coming in and out the whole day. She swept the floor, beat the red couch with a broom handle to raise the dust and washed and dried the glass teacups. She boiled water, arranged the tea set on a tray, and covered it with white muslin.

Mrs Phindi awoke before the sun rose and finished packing. She then carried two cardboard suitcases to the edge of the camp — one for her clothes, the other for knitting. Some friends helped carry the bed. It was brought to the pavement and turned upside down with the legs sticking in the air. Mrs Phindi piled the two stools, the folding chair, the cabinet and most of her other possessions inside the frame. She walked over to the relief tent to get a plastic tarp and fastened it with twine to the legs of the bed. Then she went to find her dog Lion, a thin, yellow-haired part German Shepherd which had been with her for three years. When she found him drinking from a pool, she took twine, fashioned a collar and walked him over to a crowd of women singing hymns.

MR PLAATJIE SPEAKS

The scattered skirmishes between squatters and police converged into a major confrontation shortly after midday. The blacks, dressed in khaki pants, shapeless dresses and worn suit jackets, stood near the road a few inches from a white police line. The squatters were armed with stones, sticks, bottles, broken pieces of glass, and a few knives. The police carried billy clubs and guns and dogs were stationed at regular intervals down the line. Mr Plaatjie, who stood near the front, told me later, 'To us when we looked at them, we knew what would make them mad. But they couldn't tell what we would do. That is why they were a little scared, even with their guns.' The wild, jagged movements of the squatters contrasted dramatically with the military stance of the policemen.

Mrs Phindi stood with Lion behind the front row. When the woman next to her began to sing, she joined in, at the same time holding her dog close to her. In the middle of the hymn, the police moved forward a few feet. 'We don't like it when they sing, because we don't know what they are singing,' a policeman later told a reporter.[3] Suddenly, Lion lunged for one of the Alsatians. Mrs Phindi dropped the twine. The dog's handler was caught off guard. For two or three minutes the dogs fought to a draw, each trying to pin the other under its front legs, while the policeman circled the two animals attempting to drag them apart. He finally grabbed his dog's leather leash and yanked him away. This gave Lion the advantage. He leapt and caught the Alsatian on the leg as the constable tried to keep control. The policeman found a stone and hurled it at Lion's ribs, then ran with his dog to a van. Lion was knocked down.

The fight further excited the crowd. A man standing next to Mr Plaatjie raised his knobkerrie and started to charge forward, provoking a dog to attack him with the gestures of his free hand. He then headed directly towards a tall policeman with a thick moustache and black hair. Mr Plaatjie swivelled and grabbed the man's right leg. Another person joined him and they tackled the man to the ground. When Mr Plaatjie was back on his feet, he tried to decide whether to address and calm the crowd. After all the suspicion of the last month, would they listen to him? Might it not be better if there *was* a real fight?

After ten minutes of this debate with himself, he stepped in front of the crowd, turned his back to the police, raised his hands, and spoke in Xhosa at the top of his voice. He heard himself saying that most of the people knew who he was and what he had tried to do at the camp. He knew that people had distrusted him because he was labelled a coloured, but he was still with them.

He had not left. People could go over to his house and see that it was standing there, just as before. Nothing had even been taken out. He then pointed to the bulldozer and said that it could not be stopped now. Even if they attacked the police, it would still continue to work. It was bad enough that their houses had been taken, he said, but should they let the police have their lives too?

The crowd gradually became quiet and listened. Mr Plaatjie kept his arms raised for almost five minutes. When he finally dropped them, the mood of the crowd eased. Even the police, who had not understood Mr Plaatjie's speech, were aware that the tension had broken. They began to disperse and back off. The squatters had won that confrontation, but the victory meant that the police would be able to take Modderdam without bullets.

FIRST FIRES

The burning of Modderdam began shortly after the crowd dispersed. The fire started in an empty shack at the back of the camp. A strong southeastern wind bellowed the flames and lifted the black smoke. Another blaze appeared a few minutes later at the centre of the camp. Several squatters were running towards it, feeding the flames with sticks and rotting lumber. Others who still had not evacuated their possessions from the area were running towards the pavement even more frenetically than before. The spread of the fire was checked because underbrush had been pulled from the sand long ago. But nonetheless, there were soon flames coming from all sections of the camp. Through the filter of ashes, dust and sand, Modderdam looked jarringly like a village under enemy fire, with the social work students running between the lines like Red Cross volunteers. Some squatters had begun to walk away from the camp, up the railroad bridge, with suitcases on their heads and in their arms. They did not stop at the BAAB van for a railroad ticket nor did they wait for buses. They just walked. A few others loaded their goods onto trucks parked on the far side of Modderdam Road. I helped one of the men lift a bed into the back. He and a few other men had spent the night rounding up vehicles in the township, he said. He was going to put his furniture and his family in a room in Guguletu, and he himself would go back to the hostels. Along the railroad tracks on the far side of the camp ten families clustered on the slopes that abutted the track. They sat apart from each other, barricaded by cardboard boxes and bundles of clothes wrapped in sheets. A policeman in an unmarked car patrolled the track.

Fire engines arrived an hour after the fire began. The sight of one government vehicle working to save a shack so that it could be knocked down by another only angered the squatters further.

There were many reports of the squatters setting fire to their homes during the next few days. Henry Geyser and Mike Mackenzie of the *Argus* spotted two men dragging a piece of burning cardboard to an empty shack. 'We followed the men and from a distance saw them entering several shanties.[4] Shortly afterwards smoke began pouring from them.' One of the men told the two reporters, 'We have made fires in a lot of huts and we will carry on doing it.' Asked why, the man replied, 'These people [the officials] take the wood and iron and sell it. It doesn't belong to them. That's why we are burning the place down.'

Many of the squatters and social workers reported that policemen had also set fire to the shanties. They told stories similar to those of the Werkgenot squatters whose camp had been raided two years earlier. Mrs Phindi went to inspect her shack after seeing flames nearby. As she approached, she saw a policeman walking out of the front door with a plastic bottle of methylated spirits. She stood watching until she saw flames at the front window. The man turned to her and said in Afrikaans, 'Now, where is your God?' Mrs Phindi replied that he shouldn't worry because the God of the Africans has a *very* long memory. While it was difficult to tell whether the squatters or the police took the lead in lighting the fires, it is clear that both groups worked to burn down the camp. The flaming shanty was simultaneously a strong sign of resistance and of domination. Thus each side tried to claim the symbol while blaming the other side for creating it.

When Mr Matthews returned to Modderdam in the late afternoon, he climbed a hill at the back of the camp, but could see hardly anything but smoke. He walked to his house and found what he thought had been his roof piled on top of what had been the walls. He started yanking the sheets apart and stamping on them with both feet. He was pleased to uncover an old deep-bowled pipe which he had lost a few weeks earlier. He dusted it off with his shirt tail, stuck it in his mouth and walked over to the Plaatjie's house. Mr Plaatjie was on his hill, together with a group of men in long grey coats. From the bottom of the hill the group looked like a war 'impi' come to town. The police wanted them on the ground, where they would not appear threatening. 'Come down! You are black power,' one shouted in Afrikaans.

'Where are we supposed to go,' Mr Plaatjie said. 'You have knocked down our houses and chased us here.'

Speaking through a bullhorn, one policeman warned the squatters that his men would soon charge. They mounted the hill with dogs five minutes later and the squatters retreated. Yet when the police descended, the squatters again occupied the hill. They played this game several times to sustain their spirit.

The day's fighting ended with teargas. The first cannisters were lobbed into a crowd of chanting women. More were soon launched at students. There was little panic. People ran to the pavement where they doused their faces in water from plastic jugs. They then rejoined the demonstration. Mrs Phindi was standing only a few feet from one explosion. She ran to the ISD caravan, stripped off the green scarf she was wearing on her head, soaked it in water and let the cloth dry on her stinging skin. The strong winds made it hard to aim the gas. Babies suffered the most. Many were brought choking and vomiting with heavily swollen faces to the doctors. The gas, however, seemed almost an afterthought. For by the time it spread over the camp, the outcome of the day's operations was determined, and the squatters' protest had shifted from an attempt to save Modderdam to a cathartic interlude which would make it possible for the people to scatter and move on.

That evening a protest meeting was held at St Xavier's Church in the white suburb of Claremont. Priests, ministers, and others had come to decide whether anything further could be done. The debate was tense and anxious because many felt themselves pushed further into illegal defiance than they had ever wanted to go. They saw clearly that unless some physical attempt was made to obstruct the bulldozer, all the speeches and letters to the press would mean very little. Many felt that they had let down or misled the squatters by allowing them to believe that the camp could be saved. The need to decide immediately on a form of protest helped move the group to adopt a plan it might have rejected on further reflection. They would build a human chain the next morning in front of the bulldozer and force the police to drag them away.

Later that night, the staff of CFCIA organized over a proposal to help evacuate the camp. It was possible to mass trucks and drivers, find storage space for the squatters' possessions, and obtain emergency shelter for a few days. More and more women with young children were already being taken to the hospital. Gale winds and possible rain was forecast for Wednesday. Yet they realized that by helping the squatters leave, they too were 'doing the government's dirty work.' It would make it easier for other camps to be demolished. The meeting ended without a decision.

At the camp itself, I met an African student from Guguletu. He said that he and a few of his friends had been in the camp throughout the day, helping people empty and burn the shacks. They had come in small numbers because they didn't want any security policemen to recognize them. Some had dressed up in the baggy clothes usually worn by migrants. He thought that because the squatters had been attacked, it would be easier for the students to work with them in the future. The squatters now understood more about 'the system'. The people in the bread and soup line queued till late into the night. Wendell Pietersen, a lecturer in Social Work at UWC, was stationed in the caravan with a student, Theresa Abrams. At about 11.00 p.m., a woman knocked on the door and told them that her neighbour was about to give birth. Mr Pietersen, who had taken a first-aid course some years before, took a doctor's bag that had been left in the caravan and went with Theresa to a plastic lean-to. It was lit by a paraffin lamp. The woman was already in labour. It was too late to bring her to the hospital. Her contractions grew more intense for an hour. Finally, the head appeared. Mr Pietersen's hands shook as he put one hand on the top and one hand on the bottom of the head and began to tug gently. He was surprised at how easily the body came into his hands. It was a girl. He fastened two clamps on the umbilical cord a few inches from each other and cut it in the middle. He then took the baby in his hands, held her against his chest and spanked her. She cried. Mr Pietersen lifted her into her mother's waiting arms. Later that night, he drove them to the hospital.

148

14. The Squatters Disperse

The final days of the demolition coincided with the first anniversary of the student revolt. Yet whereas in 1976 the demonstrations had spread from one end of the country to the other, this time they did not travel the few miles from Modderdam to the neighbouring townships. It was as though the government had chosen this week to test its success in dividing the different generations of Cape Town Africans. It had won its gamble at least in the short run. Symbolic protests, impotent acts of rage, and stirring memorials were the only responses left to the protesters.

DAVID RUSSELL

The full force of the gale hit early on Wednesday morning, blowing many of the plastic shelters into the road. One hundred clergymen arrived at 6.00 a.m. dressed in long robes and overcoats. They walked up Mr Plaatjie's hill and waited. They were joined by groups of squatters. The bulldozer did not come. Most of the ministers left by 9.00 a.m., although a few were left behind to warn the others should the operation begin later in the day. Many of the demonstrators thought that informers had been at the church meeting the night before, and that the government was just waiting them out. The squatters sat in front of fires all morning. It was hard to do any packing amidst the stinging sand.

The fires started again at midday. The flames spread more rapidly than the day before. Soon after, two bulldozers arrived. As they took up their positions in the camp, three white men —

Richard De Satga, John Oppleton, and David Russell walked into the camp. Police Constable H C Bernard followed. As soon as the three protesters reached the first truck, Rev Russell — the Anglican priest who had been working in the Crossroads squatter camp since its inception — calmly lay down in front of it.

He heard shouts a few seconds later — 'Vat hom, vat hom!' (grab him, grab him!) — and two policemen picked him up by his arms and legs and carried him towards the road. As he neared a police van, Rev Russell remembered that his mother's car was parked in Belhar and that she had errands to run later in the day. Seeing a friend, Mrs Moira Henderson, he twisted an arm free, pulled the keys from his pocket, and flipped them to her as he attempted to turn onto his back. He was later charged with resisting arrest and trespassing. Mr De Satga and Mr Oppleton were arrested for trespassing as well. Rev Russell later explained his actions during the trial. 'It was a spontaneous kind of thing. I believe in normally obeying the law, but as a Christian there comes a time when there is a confrontation with God's laws. Over the years I've tried to work with African families and promote a family among the people. Homes were being demolished and instead of writing another letter to those in authority, I had to use my body where communication and words were useless, as an act to uphold and be a witness to God's law. Just by obeying God's law and acting according to my conscience, I felt I could communicate to these people in power and towards people's hearts so that they could be made aware of the evil being done there.'

After the arrests the camp was closed to all whites except for a few volunteers and journalists. The new fires and the two bulldozers moved the demolition along very quickly. It appeared as if the operation would be completed by the end of the day. At about 4.00 p.m., one of the bulldozers was within an hour of the Plaatjie's shack. Mr and Mrs Plaatjie stood in front of the entrance with their arms crossed. They still had not begun to empty the shack. Every time someone offered to help, they shook their heads. Squatters and social workers nervously watched the husband and wife. No one had ever seen them so tense and furious. People feared that Mr Plaatjie, usually so restrained, might suddenly become wild and violent.

Yet finally, when the bulldozer was only three shacks away, the Plaatjies jumped up and started stripping the shack. A crowd of almost two dozen men and women rushed to help. The kitchen table came first, then the pots and dishes, the bed, the radio, and the chairs. Someone ripped down the pink curtain over the arched window in the living room. The puffy couch, the last piece of furniture to go, was pushed through the kitchen door fifteen minutes after the evacuation had begun. It was dragged, along with all the other contents of the house, to the pavement.

The bulldozer arrived at the shack at 4.30 p.m. It crashed easily through the fence, then stalled briefly in the sand as it moved uphill to the kitchen. It penetrated the shack to the bedroom, then backed up the hill and charged into the living room. When the last wall had fallen, Mrs Plaatjie threw a chair onto Modderdam Road. It bounced three times and landed in front of a green Volkswagen which swerved to avoid it. Mr Plaatjie soon joined her, winging two more chairs into the traffic. More squatters joined in, hurling their tin cans, tables, and even their clothes onto the road. Finally Mr Plaatjie, his face contorted, picked up the couch by its legs and told a man standing next to him to help. They lifted it to their chests, then heaved it. It rolled once and landed upside down in the right-hand lane. The police halted traffic as the rain of furniture continued. After about 20 minutes the Plaatjies, exhausted, began to pull their things off the road. Three chairs were broken, and the arm of the couch was ripped.

The shacks were almost all down yet most of the people were still at Modderdam. The battles with the police had eased. The squatters' rage was momentarily sapped. The full impact of homelessness began to set in. People marched up to the relief tent and demanded, 'Where are we to go? Where are we to go?' Community workers realized that this was their moment to embarrass the government. The full cruelty and stupidity of the demolition would finally emerge if the government was forced to make mass arrests or deportations, they said. Mr Matthews, who had spent the night at Unibel, warned that the time had passed to make such a last stand. Many of the committee members had already left, and the spirit of Modderdam was now broken. Unless CFCIA and ISD helped to evacuate people, the squatters who remained would panic in the cold and in the rain which was soon expected.

The community workers decided to find shelter for women and children in church halls and to store possessions in an empty Pepsi-Cola warehouse at the nearby industrial park in Epping.

When the police left at 5.00 p.m., the camp once again changed hands. Large trucks moved in and were quickly loaded. Volunteers received permission to bring people to St Monica's Convent in Elsie's River. They would be allowed to spend the night there, but would have to return to Modderdam during the day when the dormitories became a nursery school.

As I was helping to load one truck, I came across the African student I had met the day before. He said that he and his friends had their own plans. They were bringing about a hundred squatters to I D Mkize High School in Guguletu and would guard them in the classroom. They would order the businessmen in Guguletu to give them enough supplies to feed them well.

Squatters and volunteers worked until 3.00 a.m. I drove to Tygerberg Hospital in the early evening to pick up a woman who had been taken there the day before complaining of pains in her chest. Driving back to the camp, she said that she had been told to take medicine and stay in bed for two weeks. When she objected that she was from Modderdam, the doctor had told her, 'That is not my problem.'

Upon returning to Modderdam, I found Mr Plaatjie sitting in front of a fire. His wife, he said, had left for her parents' place at Factreton: his children had gone there at the beginning of the week. Mr Matthews had returned to Unibel. Mrs Phindi had been brought to the convent.

At the warehouse where the remains of the camp were being stored, each family's possessions took up about five square feet. It was very hard to distinguish one pile from another. Occasionally a bicycle or an old sewing machine would mark a more prosperous squatter. A white student was stationed there, carefully recording the location of each family's goods — all of which had been tagged at the camp. While the squatters were expected to pick up their things within the next few weeks, it seemed more likely that little would be claimed. The interior of the old Pepsi-Cola building would serve for a time as a hidden monument to Modderdam.

AN INHUMANE TASK

The BAAB officials marked Thursday with a show of benevolence.

Twelve shacks which housed the sick and the new-born were spared. Mr P S Pietersen heard the cries of two-week-old Sylvia Maganise in a shack which was about to be pushed over. When he discovered the baby in her mother's arms, he grabbed Sylvia in his own arms and said, 'I cannot push a hut down that has somebody like this in it. God knows it's an inhumane task but I'm trying to make it as humane as possible.

The camp thinned to fewer than five hundred people. Not many squatters, however, had returned to the Transkei or Ciskei. The government stated that only twenty people had accepted railroad tickets. One newspaper reported that some of those who had taken them were trying to sell them elsewhere in the city. BAAB officials confidently predicted that many of the squatters would leave at the weekend. Yet despite this assurance, the government took several preventive measures against new shanties. Army recruits from the Wingfield military camp were brought to Modderdam to search the bushes. They found a few squatters under sheets of plastic with almost no food or belongings. One recruit told a student at the University of Cape Town that some of the searchers were 'so disgusted that they refused to do their work and went back to camp.' Policemen throughout the Peninsula were reported to be on the lookout for Modderdam residents. Sightings were reported in abandoned buildings in the old coloured quarter, District Six, and on the slopes of Table Mountain overlooking Hout Bay.

MEMORIALS

Once the camp's resistance had been broken, the police no longer seemed to care if whites wandered onto the land. On Thursday evening I picked up Mrs Phindi and drove her to St Monica's Convent. She said that she had loaded most of her furniture into one of the trucks the night before, and had taken only a suitcase and a few utensils to the convent. The women, she said, all slept together in a large room. During the night, two went into labour and were rushed to the hospital. She had left her dog Lion in the camp with her friend Rita Massey who was spending the night under a plastic tarp. Tomorrow, she said, she would have to hitch a ride to Guguletu to drop Lion off at her brother's place. She also had to bring her woollen hats, which were now finished, and sell them.

Mr Plaatjie returned to Modderdam early Friday evening, 'just for a visit.' He said he had spent all of Thursday building a shack. Well, he admitted, not exactly a shack. He had tacked a little room with plastic walls onto his wife's parents' place. On a walk through the now-silent camp we were surprised to see many vegetable gardens intact amidst the debris. Near the railroad tracks, someone yelled Mr Plaatjie's name. Suddenly he laughed, waved his hand and pointed to a half-completed two-storey house at the edge of Belhar. Three squatters were waving out of a large second-floor window.

There were three services on Sunday to commemorate the camp. At Unibel, white, coloured and African ministers prayed at the shanty town's largest church. Sixty people were able to fit inside and two hundred outside. A prayer was offered for Rev Russell, still in jail because bail had been offered to him only on condition that he would enter no more squatter camps. He had refused. Punch was served after the sombre service and the Unibel committee organized a tour of the camp for those whites who were visiting for the first time.

The second gathering was at the City Hall in the centre of the city. An integrated crowd of two thousand whites, coloureds and Africans packed the large, domed auditorium. Squatters from Werkgenot, Unibel, and Modderdam were on the platform next to the Catholic and Anglican bishops of the city, the Muslim imam, Rabbi Alan Siegal of Green Point Synagogue, and Allan Boesak, a minister in the coloured division of the Dutch Reformed Church. A tall African man with a full beard, introduced as Mr Gijani of Unibel, appealed to the government through a web of Biblical quotations which he recited in Xhosa by heart. Dr Boesak received a standing ovation when he said, with evangelical flourish, that he would pray every morning and night for the downfall of the Nationalist government. The mood of the occasion, however, was best captured by Rabbi Siegal. He told a story from the Talmud of a prophet who comes to a city and begins to preach in the streets, telling the people to repent. He attracts a modest following the first week. The second week, he loses half the crowd, and the third week, only twenty people come to listen. His last follower stops coming after two months, yet for the next year he preaches daily. Finally, one citizen asks him whether he realizes that he has no audience. 'Of course I do,' the Prophet answers. 'Then why do you continue to speak?' 'I do it,' the Prophet said, 'in order that I, too, am not corrupted.'

Final prayers for Modderdam that day were said at the camp itself. The police had warned that any one still on the pavement by Monday would be arrested. The social work students were packing up the caravan. Shortly before leaving, they sat down with the remaining ten people who they were going to take to a nearby church. They held hands, sang several hymns and closed with the African National Anthem. It had begun to drizzle, and shortly after the caravan was driven over the kerb and onto Modderdam Road the rain became heavy. It did not stop until morning.

15. Wandering

One week after the evacuation of Modderdam, whites began to ask where the squatters had gone. BAAB had distributed only sixty rail passes. Twenty families had been allowed into the legal camp, KTC. Another six hundred were being housed by church and community groups throughout the city. Brigadier van der Westhuizen claimed that most of the others had returned either to the hostels or to their country homes. Railroad tickets had not been picked up, he said, because many people preferred to make the journey by car, truck, or bus. His 'sources' had sighted scores of vehicles filled with Africans driving east along the national road.

Squatters with whom I spoke agreed that the hostels were now full, although with entire families, not single migrants. They said that almost all the residents were still in Cape Town — if not in the hostels, then as lodgers in township homes or at Unibel and other squatter camps. Although I was unable to visit those staying in the townships, I did spend time at Unibel, KTC, and St Thomas's, the church which was harbouring the largest number of Modderdam refugees.

The committee at Unibel allowed people to move into their camp as long as they did not erect new shacks. Every day, inspectors went through the camp warning people that the bulldozer would soon arrive there as well. As much as the people of Unibel sympathized with those from Modderdam, they could not afford to provoke the government further with new shanties. The camp's committee appeared to have more control than that at Modderdam, even though the shanty town was larger. Mr Matthews and others from Modderdam were in demand at Unibel because the committee wanted to hear their advice and learn from the mistakes made at Modderdam. This attention helped sustain their spirit even though they soon expected to move again. One battle followed another, preventing them from giving up.

I visited KTC with a group of white and coloured SHELTER volunteers. The charity had decided to help these squatters, but not those at Unibel, because KTC was a legal camp. The SHELTER volunteers had come to help the squatters put up shacks. They had brought with them strong, brand-new corrugated iron sheets which were pre-cut and pre-stapled onto sturdy beams. A solid shanty could be erected simply by pushing together and joining the four walls.

   Shortly after we had arrived, Dennis Herbert, a SHELTER director who lived at Belhar, approached one man and offered him a new shack. The man said no, he had his own materials and would rather do it himself. He said, however, that he could use a few beams, as his own were rotting. Mr Herbert gave him four and then supervised their installation. He chided the man for not digging the holes for the posts deeply enough or spacing them properly. The man said that he wanted to build two rooms — a bedroom and a sitting room — but Mr Herbert laughed and said, 'No, one will be enough for now. You can't be too particular. You can always put up a second one later.' The man worked with the volunteers for about an hour, arguing about the construction of the walls and the roof. He then left without notice and did not return the whole afternoon. 'Well at least now we can finish the job quickly,' Mr Herbert said.

The squatters at St Thomas's were in tents on the lawn between the parish hall and the Gothic chapel. They had arrived on the night of August 16 from the convents, African high schools, and community centres, and had helped to put up large green canvas tents bought by CFCIA and a Jewish youth group. The tents were laid out in neat rows. On the first night, 200 people slept inside them. Forty were in the parish hall, and 29 men slept in a small storage building behind it. The following morning the Acting Medical Officer of Cape Town, Mr Allan Chaimowitz gave his approval. 'At this point,' he said, 'there appears to be no danger to the health of occupants in the surrounding area.

That Sunday many of the squatters attended services. Although the church was not segregated, most of the squatters sat in one section. The minister, Christopher Grigorowski, did not refer specifically to the visitors yet in his sermon celebrating 'Compassion Week', he spoke of Christ's command to shelter the homeless.

Afterwards, several young boys played soccer with a few of the Modderdam men. A few of the boys also brought food parcels for the squatters, which they deposited in the Parish Hall.

The relocation of the Modderdam squatters was soon overshadowed by the government's announcement that Werkgenot would be bulldozed for the second time in three years. BAAB officials came to the camp with a bullhorn on Monday, August 15, telling the people that their homes would be demolished on Friday unless the squatters took the shacks apart themselves. The small camp, which had had no committee, quickly organized one with the assistance of workers from ISD and an independent community organization, the Foundation for Social Development, which had not been closely involved in Modderdam. The time was so short, and resistance within Werkgenot appeared so weak, that the two groups tried simply to locate the sickest people in the camp, and provide cardboard boxes to help people pack.

The squatters did not take down their homes, and on August 24 a front-end loader prepared a path into the well-hidden camp. According to one squatter, Stanford Matyuza, a BAAB official with a rifle in one hand and spare bullets in the other had warned people that the shacks could be demolished 'at any time'. Mr Matyuza, apparently unaware of how uncompromising the government had been at Modderdam, told a reporter, 'We want the authorities to give us a year to get out of the camp.'

Werkgenot was flattened on August 25. The government first sealed off the area to all but a few reporters and photographers. It denied ISD's request to bring their first-aid caravan into the camp and ordered it to be placed on the road, a quarter of a mile away. BAAB officials accused the social work students and volunteers of having induced the squatters to stay longer at Modderdam by continuing to feed them bread and soup.

The squatters put up little fight. The only person arrested was Dr Margaret Nash, a lay officer in the Episcopal Church. She came to Werkgenot bearing a large white cross. When policemen blocked her path, she raised the cross high and walked up to her waist in the muck of the stagnant pond in front of the shacks. After she had marched to the other side, she was escorted to a police van. By 4.30 in the afternoon, only a few toilet sheds were left standing. That evening, squatters were evacuated by volunteers as they had been at Modderdam. Possessions were once again brought to the Pepsi-Cola warehouse, and squatters to church halls. This time, however, the ministers were much less enthusiastic about providing shelter. Not only did it disrupt the other activities of the church, they said; it also delayed the squatters' eventual homelessness. Yet nonetheless there were over fifteen hundred squatters scattered throughout white and coloured Cape Town.

Five families moved into tents on the grounds of St George's Cathedral in the centre of Cape Town during the first week of September. Their tents looked onto the Gardens with its great trees, ornate flower patterns and patriotic statues erected where van Riebeeck had cultivated his vegetable garden upon landing at De Kaap in 1652. The squatters quickly became the central attraction in the park — overshadowing Parliament, the great Synagogue of Cape Town and the National Art Museum. Mr Gustav Cuthelele, a dock worker, stayed in one tent with his two year-old child and his thirty-six-year-old wife, Nokyala, who was eight months pregnant. Mr Simon Joyai, in a neighbouring tent, worked as a blockman in a local butchery. His wife, Buyiswa, said, 'I came to Cape Town to be with my husband so we could have a family life. I also moved because there is very little money in Transkei. We needed money to put our children through school and we would like to stay in Cape Town.'

HAVE WE GONE MAD?

The National Party publicly debated the demolitions throughout August and September. Joyce Waring, a Nationalist journalist, asked in a guest column in the *Argus*, 'Have we all gone mad?' and confessed that 'as a Nationalist, I am ashamed.' She did not, however, protest the bulldozing itself but the government's laxness in permitting the camp to be built in the first place. 'If the law does not allow a man to come in from the Transkei or Ciskei without a permit in order to work here, why and how did these people get into the Republic? Here is a breach of the law, a laxity for which someone must shoulder the blame. The issue in this case is not whether there is work in the homelands for these people or not. The point is, why were they allowed in at all?' The squatters were part of the 'flood' of Africans which the government had pledged to staunch. Instead, she complained, 'twenty families became two hundred and then four thousand — four thousand families that put down roots, elected councils to help organize the area, and in spite of rumblings and mumblings from Ministers Marais Steyn and M C Botha (Minister of Bantu Affairs) decided that they were here to stay.' As a result, the government was forced into the embarrassing demolition and opened itself to the self-righteous cries of the moralists. 'I am tired of being asked by callers on my telephone, "How do you feel sleeping in your warm bed when you know what is happening to those unfortunate squatters at Modderdam?"' Mrs Waring asked rhetorically how she, 'as a humanitarian as well as a Nationalist' should reply. 'Sometimes, as now, I find it very difficult to know where I stand.'

A correspondent to *Die Burger* complained of the timing of the demolition. 'As a lifelong Nationalist and active office-bearer of the National Party I make an urgent appeal to the Government to stop the clearing of squatter areas in the Cape until after winter, except where other reasonable accommodation is available.' The New Dutch Reformed Church, which had ceded part of the land on which Modderdam had been built to the government in order to facilitate the demolition, had a similar criticism. An editorial in its official newspaper, *Die Kerkbode,* conceded that 'One's Christian conscience and sense of fellow-humanity is involuntarily stirred at the realisation that the shacks of black squatter families were destroyed before the severe Cape winter had reached its end.' The squatters, the editorial said, wished to have protection under a roof and not be exposed 'to the blows of the elements', as does 'everyone of us'. 'We also believe that the work which the officials concerned had to perform could not have been done without unpleasantness. Therefore it is to be regretted that this particular time was chosen for the demolitions. That was why much more emotionalism and greater hysteria arose than might otherwise have been the case.'

One of the few direct attacks from within the National Party came from theological students at the Afrikaans-speaking University of Stellenbosch. In a letter to *Die Burger* the students said: 'It is with dismay that we have followed the way in which the squatter problem has been handled and especially the demolition of their homes.' The students felt a 'paralysing fear' which led them to pray, 'God forgive us, because we know not what we have done.'

The official response to this dissent within the National Party was given by Secretary of Bantu Affairs, Wilhelm Cruywagen, during a caucus of the entire party in the Cape Town City Hall the day before Werkgenot fell: 'I am very sorry that it [the Modderdam demolition] occurred this way, but how else could it have been done? We did not have any other way.' Mr Cruywagen also said that he regretted that the operation was conducted in winter but argued that 'the longer you wait, the worse the problem becomes and in the end, you may never be able to control it.' He went on to point out that the well-constructed paths in the camp and the internal organization were signs that the squatters themselves were not the people who cared the most about Modderdam. 'It is quite apparent that there were other hands behind it. Of that I have not the slightest doubt.'

When the squatters were placed in the centre of Cape Town, the accuracy of Mr Cruywagen's charge was confirmed for many Nationalists. *Die Burger* protested, 'All gullible souls who had thought that it (the housing of squatters) was a case of showing humaneness to the destitute — even if it was the kind of neighbourly love that is broadcast from street corners — will know now that they have been misled. The tents have nothing to do with Christ and morality. The aim is to point a finger at the authorities and the public. It is a chattering on the street for the sake of naked politicizing.' The erecting of the tents was, *Die Burger* charged, 'a defiant act that does not take any account of the legal implications. And this we find the most shocking of all.' The paper asked what the consequences would be if blacks inferred from it that illegal protest is sanctioned by the church. 'We are putting it mildly when we say that it is playing with fire to protest this way in South Africa.'

LIBERALS

White opponents of the National Party reacted to the demolition with sarcasm, a new awareness of their own impotence, calls for civil disobedience, and in a few cases, support for violent revolution. Helen Suzman, a Progressive-Reform member of Parliament, was encouraged that Joyce Waring had condemned the government's clumsy handling of Modderdam, but added, 'What Mrs Waring should also condemn is the disgusting policy which lies at the root of this typically callous action by the government she supports.' Dr van Zyl Slabbert, the member of parliament who had supported the squatters strongly during the House of Assembly debates, reported to his constituency that the razing of Modderdam was 'the most premeditated and calculated event that I can think of . . . The script for this macabre social drama was meticulously prepared in Parliament.'

The *Cape Times* mocked *Die Burger's* expression of outrage at the Church's willingness to house squatters. 'Some people shock more easily than others. There are many thousands less shocked by a handful of tents in public view than they are by the destruction of countless shacks before the occupants have alternative accommodation . . . Such official action is not defiant, just inhuman.' Privately, members of the staff questioned the value of the editorial support they had given the people of Modderdam, and of the SHELTER fund the newspaper had founded and helped to administer. 'I'm afraid we learned more from Modderdam than the squatters did,' one editor said to me.

Mr Matthews settled in quickly at Unibel. When I spoke to him in early September he talked with the enthusiasm of a politician long deprived of an audience. He had quickly mastered the intricacies of the politics and rivalries of the committee, which were as complex as those at Modderdam. He was most interested in the recent departure of one of the senior members of the camp — the tall, bearded man who had spoken so eloquently at the protest in the City Hall. Shortly after that meeting, Mr Matthews said, the man, Mr Ginyani, was visited by two members of the Special Branch. They offered him a plot at KTC and offered his wife special permission to stay in Cape Town. Mr Ginyani at first refused. The following week, however, the employer in the shop where he had worked for twenty years told him that he would be fired if he did not move to KTC. Mr Ginyani, who was to receive his pension in a few years, changed his mind.

Mr Matthews also spoke of a young woman staying in the camp who had been on the front lines during the most violent days of the Guguletu uprising. Before Modderdam had been knocked down, Mr Matthews said, her opinions would have been ignored. Now it was as though they were hanging on her words. Mr Matthews said he was not bitter over his treatment by the squatters at the end of the campaign. 'I am mad at Tala,' he said, 'but not at the others, really. People were scared and they didn't know what to do, so they just fought with each other.' Mr Matthews said he had heard that Mr Tala had also been given a shack at KTC. (When I visited that camp a second time I found him. Mr Tala greeted me like an old friend and said he liked his new place.)

I asked Mr Matthews to compare Modderdam to Retreat, the camp he had won twenty years ago. He laughed. 'It was so much easier then. The superintendent there was really quite a reasonable chap. But these boys today . . . ' His voice trailed off as he shook his head. As he said goodbye, I asked him about his plans. 'Oh, I'll be staying somewhere in these bushes. I want to see how it all works out.'

Mr Plaatjie became seriously depressed in the weeks after the demolition. He spent much of the morning in bed. He stopped reading the newspapers. He took long walks by himself in the streets of Factreton, and seldom spoke of Modderdam. Several times he had made weak efforts to look for jobs, but he stalled until it was too late in the day to apply. He was worried in part that employees might learn of his role in the camp and that he would then be blacklisted as an agitator.

Mrs Plaatjie adjusted with less visible strain. When I visited her parents' house, she was working at the kitchen table handing out orders as she had done at Modderdam. She said with a laugh that she was now sorry she had broken all those chairs when she threw them into the road.

I visited the Plaatjies one evening to show them pictures of the destruction. The house was crowded, and drunk people kept walking in and out of the door yelling at each other. Mr Plaatjie looked at the photographs and said 'Modderdam' quietly to himself several times before wrapping them carefully in a paper napkin and pressing them in a Bible. I then reminded him of a promise he had once made to me at the camp — that he would take me to the horse races. He smiled, agreed, and set a date for the following Saturday.

We drove out to the track at Kenilworth on a warm spring day with ten rands between us. At the end of the day we came out ahead by four rands. He laughed when I threatened to expose the leader of the squatters as a gambler. 'Don't worry,' he said, 'if I ever win the jackpot, I'll build myself the biggest pondokkie in Cape Town.'

Mrs Phindi was moved from St Monica's Convent to St Thomas's a few days after her shack had been burned down. She was put in a tent with her friend Rita Massey. Each woman had a small cot. Mrs Phindi had with her a suitcase and a few cooking utensils. For the first few days, church volunteers cooked for the entire camp in a communal kitchen. The squatters were then given daily rations of soup, beans, corn meal, meat and other foods which they prepared themselves on Primus stoves. One day she showed me a plastic band on her arm with her name written on it — a hospital identification tag. A volunteer had snapped it on her and told her that she mustn't take it off, otherwise she would not receive her rations. It was important, the woman said, that no outsiders came for free food. Mrs Phindi complained that without her store, she had nothing to do and no way to make money. Some of the squatters now watched television in the evening or saw movies in the parish hall, but she had little patience with such 'nonsense'. She said that what she really wanted to do was to sell old clothes in the hostels. She asked me if I could collect any from friends.

The next time I visited her at St Thomas's she said, 'I've got to get out of this place.' She said she was getting tired of all the whites who had come into the camp to help them. 'They think we do not know how to do anything,' she said. 'They forget that we are the same people who go and do some washing and all that in *their* houses.' One woman had even tried to teach her how to knit! Mrs Phindi also said that she was angry at many of the squatters who were now becoming greedy. 'They give each person a towel. So then there are some who hide it, and ask for another the next day.' There were others, she said, who really *did* have other places to stay, but were just using the tents for a vacation.

She wanted to move into the hostels and set up a little store there, but she was afraid it was still too soon after the demolition to risk police raids. I asked her if she had thought of going back to Queenstown in the Ciskei. 'No. Where to? What do I do there?' she said instinctively. But a few minutes later, she reconsidered. 'I might, if I could get an old bakkie. Then maybe I could do business there. But without one it would be useless because the distances are *too* far.'

During the last week in August, Commissioner of Bantu Affairs Botha released a statement warning churchmen and private individuals who were harbouring squatters that 'the actions of do-gooders would not lead to a solution of the squatter problem. On the contrary, it strengthens the squatters in their continued disregard for the country's laws.' Mr Botha urged these 'do-gooders' to 'act positively by letting the squatters understand unambiguously that the solution to their problems lies in the use of the proffered help from the authorities to return to their places of origin.' Squatters had 'dug themselves in', Mr Botha said, only because they had received encouragement from white instigators.

Raids on churches housing squatters began on September 3. Officials of the Divisional Council arrived at St Monica's Roman Catholic Centre in the coloured township of Elsie's River at 2.00 p.m.

Ten workers began dismantling the 30 tents, which housed 230 squatters, at 3.00 p.m. Passersby shouted at them and threw stones and cried 'shame' when one tent was lifted up and a two-year-old was found sleeping underneath. One worker from ISD who had kept her temper throughout the destruction of Modderdam could no longer contain herself as she watched the men roll up the canvas and slide the tents into vans. 'I went right up to them and shouted, "Jy fokin' boer, jy fokin' boer" right in their faces. I didn't care whether they arrested me. I just didn't care.'

Mrs Phindi was woken at 4.30 a.m. on September 9 by shouting. Flashlight beams danced on the walls of her tent. Before she could try to hide, the police entered and asked both her and Mrs Massey for their passes. Although neither woman had the proper stamps, only Mrs Massey was arrested, along with 117 others who were carted away in police vans one hour later. Later in the day, Brigadier van der Westhuizen explained: 'We left behind a number at the church because we did not think it best to lock up women with children.' When the *Cape Times, The Argus,* and *Die Burger* all printed the bitter and amazed reactions of church leaders and others to the arrests, Brigadier van der Westhuizen complained that the operation was not intended as an attack on religion. 'It is being treated with great emotion. But we did not just act against people of the church. Any member of the public accommodating these people illegally must expect action to be taken.'

The following day Mrs Phindi was given R50 by Father Gregorowski to pay Mrs Massey's fine. He instructed her, and the others who were going to collect their friends and relatives, not to tell the officials that the church had donated the money because this might only increase the frequency of the arrests.

Squatters began to leave St Thomas's on September 13. Mrs Phindi decided to go to Unibel. Mr Matthews had found her a place. The raids on churches continued and by the end of the month almost all the squatters had left.

The government announced at the end of October that the story of Modderdam was over. BAAB issued this statement:

> Except for a very few families, all the people who were living in tents at church properties in the Peninsula have departed as is also the case with the black people who lived at Modderdam Road and Werkgenot, and conditions have returned to normal.
>
> Negotiations are taking place about the inhabitants of Unibel and that will, hopefully, bring an end to the problem in that area.
>
> The atmosphere created by incorrect press reports has, together with other factors, for the past two years, tended to encourage illegal influx and illegal squatting which led to the misery of thousands in those camps.
>
> Therefore it is necessary to point out that such reports still persist, recently, in spite of all efforts to solve the problem amicably.
>
> On October 14, 1977, it was again reported about the squatters that 'all but a few hundred probably are still working, living and establishing roots in the Peninsula.'
>
> In this report the following were not considered:
>
> (1) Large numbers of vehicles were seen on the road loaded with squatters and their possessions. On a Sunday afternoon more than 20 vehicles, ten of them buses, were seen on the national road.

(2) One bus company has conveyed more than 1 000 such squatters.

(3) The squatters were offered an opportunity to demolish their huts and remove the building material. Then they did not. So they had to buy new material to build again in the 'virgin' bush. A trader in second-hand building material reported that he sold about R63 000 worth of material to squatters in the past year, but that this trade has now come to a standstill.

(4) All local authorities in the Peninsula have been on the look-out for new squatter huts, which are broken down immediately, either in other camps or in the 'virgin bush'.

The statement ended with a challenge to those who believed that the squatters were still in Cape Town to bring proof to the Bantu Affairs Administration Board.

In November Mr Plaatjie found a job as a freight-lift operator at R115 a month. The fights in his wife's parents' house became more and more intense until Mr Plaatjie feared that the marriage might collapse. Finally, however, they were given a four-roomed house in Elsie's River, about a mile from Modderdam Road.

Mr Matthews and Mrs Phindi remained at Unibel until January 1978 when that camp, too, was bulldozed. The demolition was not as hazardous to the squatters as Modderdam had been since it came in the middle of summer. The government, however, had to use more force and arrest more people in order to make the squatters leave the site. After watching the police and the squatters fight one more time, Mr Matthews decided that he had had enough of Cape Town. He packed two suitcases and returned to Touws River, the village where he was born and raised. Mrs Phindi left for Queenstown to visit relatives — expecting, however, to return in a few months.

The land along Modderdam Road lay fallow. Because of all the toilets and garbage pits, the ground was well fertilized. Bushes began to grow back and the gardens which the squatters had left behind prospered. Mealie stalks planted shortly before the camp was

167

destroyed stood up tall and ears began to form. Melons, carrots, cucumbers, and a few tomatoes slowly ripened. In late February and early March, Africans were once again seen along Modderdam Road. This time, however, they did not bring zincs with them but rakes and shovels. They built small fires in front of the plots and stood guard during the night. One evening, a resident of Belhar went to visit the men as he was taking his dog for a walk. They told him that they were the people of Modderdam. They had once lived there, and now they had returned because it was time for the harvest.

FOOTNOTES

Chapter II

1. David Selvan, *Housing Conditions for Migrant Workers in Cape Town 1976*, (Cape Town, 1976).
2. Athol Fugard, Winston Ntshona, John Kani, *Sizwe Bansi is Dead*, in *Statements*, London, 1975.

Chapter IV

1. H. B. Thom, ed., *Journal of Jan van Riebeeck*, vol. III, Cape Town, 1952, p. 329.
2. *Publication of the Van Riebeeck Society*, vol. 1, pp. 136 – 137 as quoted in Eric A. Walker, *A History of Southern Africa* (London, 1965) p. 85.
3. Quoted in Walker, *A History of Southern Africa*, p. 169.
4. See Monica Wilson and Leonard Thompson, eds., *The Oxford History of South Africa*, vol. 1 (Oxford, 1969).

Chapter V

1. Francis Wilson and Dominique Perrot, eds., *Outlook on a Century* (Lovedale, 1973) p. 20.
2. Ibid.
3. Ibid., p. 96.

4.   Ibid., p. 302.

5.   O. Doughty, *Early Diamond Days* (London, 1963) p. 184 as quoted in Wilson and Thompson eds., *The Oxford History of South Africa* vol. II (Oxford, 1971) p. 181.

6.   Wilson and Perrot, eds., *Outlook*, p. 351.

7.   *Report of the Transvaal Indigency Commission.* Minutes of Evidence, p. 196. As quoted in Wilson and Thompson, eds., *Oxford History* vol. II p. 111.

8.   Report of the Economic Commission, para. 52. Quoted by S. T. van der Horst, *Native Labour in South Africa,* (Cape Town, 1942) p. 187.

9.   Transvaal, Province of, *Report of the Local Government Commission* (1921) (T.P. 1 — 1922, Pretoria, 1922).

10.   D. W. Kruger ed., *South African Parties and Policies 1910 — 1960* (Cape Town, 1960) p. 380.

11.   *Transvaal Local Government Commission,* para 42.

12.   'African Townsmen? South African Native (Urban Areas) Legislation Through the Years,' *African Affairs,* 1969, pp. 99 — 100.

13.   Kruger, *Parties and Policies.*

14.   Wilson and Perrot, eds., *Outlook*, p. 353.

15.   Ibid.

16.   Ibid., p. 357.

17.   Ibid., p. 370.

18.   Ibid.

19.   'Address to the annual conference of the Institute of Race Relations,' *Race Relations Journal,* VI, 2.

20.   J. C. Smuts, *The Basis of Trusteeship* (Johannesburg, 1942), p. 10. As quoted in Wilson and Thompson eds., *Oxford History* vol. II, p. 189.

21.   Alan Paton, *Cry the Beloved Country* (New York, 1948) p. 57.

22.   Union of South Africa, *Report of the Native Laws Commission,* 1946 — 48 (U. G. 20 — '48) para. 28.

23.   Kruger, *Parties and Policies,* p. 404.

Chapter VI

1.   See Monica Wilson and Archie Mafeje, *Langa* (Cape Town, 1963).

2.   Dr. W. W. M. Eiselen, 'The Coloured People and the Natives', *Journal of Racial Affairs,* VI, 2.

3.   Ibid., p. 11.

4.   Pelzer, A. N. ed., *Verwoerd Speaks* (Johannesburg, 1964).

5.   Muriel Horrell, *A Survey of Race Relations 1954 — 55* (Jhb., 1955).

6.   Pelzer, *Verwoerd Speaks*.
7.   Ibid.
8.   'Nyanga Emergency Camp', *South African Outlook*, July 2, 1956, p. 110.
9.   *Contact*, 21 March, 1959.
10.   *Memorandum on the Pass Laws*, (Johannesburg, 1960) pp. 31 – 37.
11.   *Die Burger*, July 9, 1962.
12.   Ibid., July 24, August 24, 1962.
13.   *Die Transvaler*, August 30, 1962.
14.   *Die Burger*, August 8, 1962.
15.   Ibid., September 9, 1962.
16.   Pelzer, *Verwoerd Speaks*.
17.   Quoted in Dr. O. D. Wollheim, 'The New Townsmen', *South African Outlook*, January 1966, p. 8.
18.   Janet Graaf and Johann Maree, 'Residential and Migrant African Workers in Cape Town,' (Cape Town, 1977).
19.   Ibid., p. 47.

Chapter VII

1.   The account of the demolitions at Werkgenot is taken from trial testimony given in the trial of Marius de Jager and Cornelius Goosen in Cape Town M Regional Magistrate's Court. Goosen and de Jager were each charged with 12 counts of malicious damage to property.
        Quotations are from the report of the trial in the *Cape Times*, March 15 – 21, 1975.
2.   *Cape Times*, April 26, 1975.
3.   The account of the Thabatha family is detailed in *South African Outlook*, April, 1976, p. 52.
4.   *Die Burger*, November 11, 1975.
5.   Excerpts from the House of Assembly debate are taken from *Hansard*, May 10, 1976, (6345 – 6428) and *Hansard*, May 17 – 18, (6864 – 6979).
6.   *Cape Times*, April 16, 1976.
7.   Ibid.

Chapter VIII

1.   *Cape Times*, 14 August, 1976.

2. The following account of the Nyanga clashes is taken fron testimony heard in Cape Town from June 7 — 30, 1977 by the Cillie Commission, as reported in the *Cape Times*.

Chapter IX

1. *Cape Times*, July 2, 1977.
2. Ibid., February 8, 1977.
3. 'Memorandum — Modderdam Road Squatters Committee,' *South African Outlook*, March 1977, p. 40.

Chapter X

1. Excerpts from the House of Assembly debate are taken from *Hansard*, February 9, 1977 (1073 — 1091) and from accounts in the *Cape Times*, February 18 — 19.
2. *Government Gazette*, June 3, 1977.
3. Excerpts from the House of Assembly debate are taken from *Hansard*, April 27, 1977 (6291 — 6333); April 28, 1977 (6335 — 6424); and May 5, 1977 (6897 — 6941).

Chapter XI

1. *Cape Times*, June 25, 1977.
2. Ibid., July 2, 1977.
3. Ibid., July 8, 1977.
4. Ibid., July 11, 1977.
5. Ibid., July 15, 1977.
6. *Die Burger*, July 26, 1977.
7. *Cape Times*, July 28, 1977.

Chapter XIII

1. *Cape Times*, August 9, 1977.
2. Ibid.
3. *Cape Times*, August 13, 1977.
4. *The Argus*, August 13, 1977.